# WRITING

# YOUR LIFE

Other Books by
**Lou Willett Stanek**


So You Want to Write a Novel
Story Starters

# WRITING YOUR LIFE

## *Putting Your Past on Paper*

L OU  W ILLETT  S TANEK, PH.D.

## Quill

*An Imprint of* HarperCollins*Publishers*

HarperCollins books may be purchased for educational, business, or sales promotional use. For information please write: Special Markets Department, HarperCollins Publishers Inc., 10 East 53rd Street, New York, NY 10022.

First Avon Books edition published 1996.

Reprinted in Quill 2002.

Library of Congress Cataloging-in-Publication Data

Stanek, Lou Willett.
    Writing your life : putting your past on paper / Lou Willett Stanek.
       p.   cm.
1. Autobiography—Authorship.  2. Stanek, Lou Willett.  I. Title.
CT25.S73      1996                                               96-19329
808'.06692—dc20                                                  CIP

ISBN 0-380-78625-7

    04 05 06 RRD 10 9 8

*To*
*Lucy Ann Geiselman*
I remember friendship

*Whatever shall we do in that remote spot? Well, we'll write our memoirs. Work is the scythe of time.*

*—Napoleon Bonaparte, on board HMS* Bellerophon,
*August 1815*

# Contents

*vii*

# Introduction

Recently I went back to the white clapboard house, square as a box of paper napkins, the place with the uneven sidewalk where, on brand-new ball-bearing roller skates, I broke my arm as soon as my father turned loose of my hand. We moved there from the farm when I was six, but I flew away from southern Illinois long ago. I doubt the house is still there.

I wanted to fly even before I realized I had to write. Swooping down from the low limb of a cherry tree any tomboy could climb, I made my first flight with a kitchen-curtain cape streaming from Wonder Woman's narrow shoulders. In the spring the fruit tree's limbs, lush with leaves and sweet-smelling blossoms, provided an umbrella to protect me from reality, while Mother and the boxy house's back door were close enough for comfort.

Anyone who physically and emotionally outlasts childhood has something to write about forever. After many successful flights, Wonder Woman crashed on her nose. Next
a frisky horse darted under a low limb. Then it was a deep
dive into the shallow end of the swimming pool. By twenty,
I had a beak like a parrot. Not even the domestic airlines
were interested in having a stewardess with a profile problem, not even Wonder Woman.

Before imposing, passenger-packed jets, when flying was
still considered glamorous, the competition for a stewardess position was ferocious. The year I applied, the probabil-
ity numbers were about as chilling as for the first
unsolicited novel I submitted to an editor. Trying to let me
down easy, the smooth airline recruiter with ersatz charm,
a slick gray suit that looked as if it had been scaled off a
fish, and a what's-a-guy-to-do expression told me they had
received 5,280 applications for 300 slots in stew classes.
Rejection is not an acquired taste. When you're young, it's
a killer. With his eye on my tears, his watch, and the next
flight out of town, the recruiter, displaying effete sympathy,
also told me about surgery that could fix my nose.

Even on a bad day, writing is more fun than having a
nose job, but not as good for one's self-esteem as flying
was in what Galway Kinnel recalls as the "heyday of stew-
ardesses" when flight attendants had a "virginal alertness."
The wings on the crisp uniform liberated me, allowing me
to fly over the confining cornfields and conservatism of my
childhood. *Or at least, that's the way I remember it.*

Writers weave myths out of memory. The surgery might
not have been as ghastly as I recall. My mother might not
have been as concerned, my father as horrified, when I
called them . . . after the deed was done. At least my father
paid the bill, if grimly. I'm sure of that.

Seasoned by time, remembrances change shape and
color. With a little help from our imaginations, desires, and
experiences, we have the power and the privilege to invent
the truth. Malleable memory, not magic, turns people,
events, and things into symbols. We reconstruct our pasts
in tune with our heart's desires to become the heroes of
our own myths.

Most of my University of Chicago colleagues found my
flying career amusing and gallantly forgave me for my frivo-

lous lapse. Frivolous? Who safely evacuated fifty-six passengers from an emergency landing in' a field? Who held Willy Mays's hand on landing and takeoff, calmed his fear of flying? I remember having serious discussions with people like Robert Oppenheimer, reading Joyce at his tower in Dublin, writing a master's paper on *The Fairie Queen* after flying a back-to-back night trip. Pitying my associates their missed opportunities for daring adventures, I pardoned their stuffiness.

We often accuse others of the shadows in ourselves.

Someone wise said language has double power to create and exorcise. I find a third dimension: to escape. I began to work on this book the week I bought a hundred-year-old neglected cottage on an island in Maine. Arriving in July after a long, hot drive from New York, I waded through weeds to my waist, opened the door, and screamed. During the winter, rapacious raccoons had exercised their squatter's rights. The water pipes and the toilets had burst. The wind and sea had dumped debris, maybe bats, through a broken window. The local paper said the night before, a boy had found a possum in his bed.

Who wanted to be there? I didn't want to be there. For this trip I did not need a plane, however. I turned on my computer and went back to southern Illinois, to the square white house where I lived when I was six, "when the livin' was easy." *Or at least, that's the way I remember it.*

But when writing about our history, the tense is always past imperfect. There is no way to regain the bulletproof vest of innocence we wore back then.

Eventually, when the experience is not so raw, I'll write about the Maine cottage. My mother would smile if she knew I had escaped . . . back home. She maintained I had begun to try to get away when I learned to crawl. My father thought the world quit at our county line, and he did not trust airplanes. When Mother told him I was going to fly, he asked her how she could let me go. Translator was her role in the family. "Because I want to keep her," my wise mother replied. Memories tie you to where you came from even if it's not the place you had in mind.

Before I had seen Barcelona or lived long enough to have much to recall, I made up sensational stories set in far-away places, casting myself in the lead as rodeo queen,

foreign correspondent, test pilot, bareback rider in the circus. On my mighty steed, Prince, I, Belle Starr, led the
Younger Gang into scandalous mischief all over our
pasture.

At school I was always in trouble. Some eight-year-old
tattletale in training to be a sycophant invariably told on
me. Hidden behind the kind of desk whose top pulled up
like a shield, I wrote down the spectacular tales I made up
and, God forbid, read stories. I think I became a writer out
of pure stubbornness. I loved to read, and someone was
always saying I couldn't or shouldn't or I was going to ruin
my eyes. I still feel guilty reading for pleasure during the
day. It's like having a drink before five.

I live in Manhattan now, go to Maine in the summer, and
spend all of my time reading, writing, and teaching. I wrote
the script in southern Illinois a long time ago. It could be
a figment of my imagination.

For several years I've taught fiction writing classes where
my students and I play a pleasurable game of pretend.
With nary a twinkle in anyone's eye, we make believe the
characters and events in everyone's story are imaginary.
There's the sensitive ironworker with a degree in English
whose responsive character is fighting for union control
of . . . the ironworkers. The restless lawyer has created an
ambitious protagonist who comes to realize life has more
to offer than winning a court case. The gay man, who at
the time didn't know how to say he was sorry, has written
a moving story about a homosexual who is able to explain
to his wife and kids why the honest way is the better way.

I've decided to go straight.

Not everyone can invent a plot convincing us Anna Karenina would have jumped in front of a moving train, and
you might not be ready to confess as Saint Augustine did
in the fourth century before news spread like the seven-
year itch, but we all have a plethora of stories. Finding the
words to tell what has happened and how you feel about
it is the way we come to understand why the world is what
it is and why things happen as they do.

So many memorable things have already happened, most
of us with other jobs and unfinished lives do not have time
to start in the beginning and work our way through the
thicket of family, friends, career, etc., as autobiographers

tend to do. Although a memoir and an autobiography are kissing cousins, the similarities can be slight.

Most autobiographies tend to spread all over your life, like a runny batter, while a memoir can be neat, tidy, and much easier to handle and contain. Imagine your life rolled out in one huge piece of dough, but what interests you at the moment is your ghastly thirteenth summer, that year when you didn't feel as if you fitted into anyone's niche. Cut out that one piece and roll the rest up for another day. Working with a small bit of your past makes it easier to keep focused.

Perhaps you will collect a potpourri of remembrance for your own pleasure, or give it to someone as a present, or send one to a magazine, or quarterly. While you are telling time, you might even find a book tucked in there with all the mishmash.

The personal memories I will share with you in search of your own are the truth, or at least the way I remember them.

Writing from memory allows you to time-travel, to zoom back to people and places you have not seen in years. Buckle your seat belt. This trip could be the exhilarating escapade you've been itching for. Learning to see when you have moved too near to Narcissus's pool, you will show how you have learned from the highs and lows, changed and grown. Prepare for having fun in the process.

# BREAKING
# THE ICE

## Chapter 1
## You Learn to Write by Writing

*Footfalls echo in the memory*
*Down the passage which we did not take*
*Towards the door we never opened*
*Into the rose garden.*

—*"Four Quartets,"* T.S. Eliot

The magic words for fiction writers are "what if . . ."; for memoir writers, "I remember . . ." breaks the ice.

Without memory, time has no meaning.

You have had an interesting, distinctive life, but who will know? Think about your heirs. Family history ranks high as a legacy. My intention in *Writing Your Life* is to help you sort out the jumble of pain, pleasure, accomplishments, and regrets you have accumulated. You know what happened. The book will encourage you to write to explore what it means, to tell others, and to enjoy this adventuresome and mysterious journey into your past.

If you were to write an autobiography, you would have to spend a lot of time at the courthouse, looking up the date your great-grandfather was born, what year your fa-

ther bought the house on Elm Street. The research for a
memoir can be done in an easy chair. Close your eyes and
try to recapture the moment you bought your first car,
learned you were pregnant, met the president, or wobbled
down the street on a two-wheeler. I am sure you can recall
initiation night, the first time you spoke in public, or the
first time you said, "I love you."

You do not have to have been a young man in Paris to
have had a life that is a "moveable feast."

Remember the first time you lied to your father and he
knew, or how silly you felt when she took that photograph
of you riding a sulky elephant in India? Who but you
knows how hellish it was to please a son of a gun with
that much power? Your first kiss, of course, you will never
forget, but don't you wonder if he has? Was there ever a
home with as many places to hide and pout as that house
you moved into the summer you were eight? Everyone
knows his account, but unless you write your version, who
will know there was another side to the family squabble or
office feud? Today you might even be brave enough to expose that pit bull of a kid who made first grade hideous.
He never left Omaha, so he can't get you, can he? And your
daughter's garden wedding when it rained; now, that was
a day to be recorded.

All of us know we are different from anyone else, and if
others only knew what we see, how we feel and think, they
would understand and appreciate us more, for pity sakes.
But until we find the language to express our view, we
don't always understand ourselves or the world we inhabit.
For me writing is a necessity. I get twitchy and cranky until
I wrestle those sensations into an image I can see, an idea
that makes sense. I write to learn what I know and how I
feel about it.

A fine artist and friend in Maine believes some responses
defy spoken language and becomes impatient when I
search for words to express how I feel about her work. So
I wait until I leave the studio to begin my probe. The experience hasn't happened, the gift she has given isn't mine,
until I can express it. Our ability to be moved by music,
art, language, brings balance to a world crammed with
crime, noise, bills, bureaucratic bother. I can't bear to leave
behind a sensation that offers a feeling of peace and brings

order, no matter how briefly, to tumbling, stumbling, trials, and troubles.

Do you remember your reaction to the piece of sculpture you discovered, quite by accident, one foggy evening in a tiny Venice courtyard? You probably said, I'll never forget this moment, I'll never be the same. Yet, unless you put some phrases on paper, no matter how hard it is finding fresh words for your feelings, the passion probably escaped, leaving no trace. Practice will make it easier.

When something happens I want to share and remember, like the morning a bull moose strolled into my backyard on Bailey Island, the first version is usually a letter. Since my pen pal list would stretch from here to Peoria, I recycle the news, altering it only to fit the receiver. My noncritical sister and my friend Lucy Ann are most apt to receive a purple prose account drowning in adjectives, slashed with exclamation points. The next interpretation usually goes to Illinois to Jane, a dream of a friend for a writer and her publisher. She bought nineteen copies of my last book. I do a translation trying understatement, irony, for Jane, who wants to be remembered for what she *didn't* say. By the time I report to an editor, a gentleman caller I'm trying to impress, writers in my workshop, or my former husband (who writes like a pro), I've hopefully tamed the beast—in this case the bull moose and the prose. I sold the strolling moose tale to a newspaper sans even one exclamation point, but that critter is still in my notebook and settling into my storehouse of tales. Don't be surprised if he charges into another story.

Eventually the moose tale will move into memory and change, of course. The letters and the news story telling who, what, where, and why were immediate reactions. Even though the islanders said there was something wrong with me and the moose when I tried to touch him and he let me, I haven't yet learned much from the experience. In a few years, the incident will linger somewhere between myth and reality. The moose will probably become bigger, I braver. Reconstructing the past is allowed, even natural. We will pursue this phenomenon of reinventing reality further in another chapter.

Of course, we will never hear the beast's view. In the newspaper story I suggested he might have a penchant for tall women in white nightgowns, but I made that up. What separates you, me, and the moose with the mournful face is our need to be heard, to be visible, to make sense of our lives. Writing grants a means of self-discovery, a way to break through to the fortitude, the idiosyncrasies, that make us unique. You and your husband might have looked out the same kitchen window for twenty years, your eyes might be as green as your uncle Harry's, but twenty bucks says you don't see the world as they do.

Start writing to save your life. Stories only happen to those who can tell them.

*Writing Your Life* issues an invitation for you to write it like it was, or the way you think it was. The request for the pleasure of your company comes with suggestions for the shortest and most pleasant way to get there from wherever you are.

Actually, the suggestions I offer for writing a memoir won't be too much different from what I say in my fiction workshops. You will be encouraged to evoke memories, re-create scenes with description and dialogue, extrapolate plots from your life, and perhaps most important, discover your own voice.

The only truth I know is, you learn to write by writing. For proof read *This Side of Paradise*, Fitzgerald's warm-up exercise for *The Great Gatsby*. I would prefer you did not read my first published works, "Lou's Teen Talk," my thirteen-year-old efforts to be Illinois's Cindy Adams in a weekly column in *The Vandalia Leader*.

Beginning right now, I implore you to become intoxicated with language. Make lists, write letters, keep a journal, take notes, jot down ideas. Talk back on paper to the TV, authors, your boss. Who will know? Scribble, doodle, and scrawl until your mind is raining words.

When we were learning to talk, those we wanted to please peppered us with praise and pats for the most ridiculous sounds. For "Da" . . . "Ma" . . . "wooo," we were told we were brilliant, a good-good girl, a William Safire in a high chair. And it worked. Most people can talk a blue streak with no problem.

Writing the same words, however, probably didn't earn you similar rewards. For many, next came what I recall as The Scarlet Fever School of Writing. Remember those redsplotched papers? On Friday afternoon in my elementary school, if there was time after we did important things like memorize the gross natural products of the countries in South America, all of us wrote an essay on titillating, sexually biased subjects like "How to Cook Spaghetti" for the girls, or "How to Change a Bike Tire" for the guys. Since I liked to ride fast horses, wouldn't have known where to find a pot in our kitchen, and thought pasta tasted like paste warmed up, my papers came back diseased, covered with scarlet spots and unrecognizable words in the margins like AWK and SP.

As a result of discouraging words received early and stored away, never to be forgotten, most writers, except Joyce Carol Oates, suffer from periodic bouts of writer's block. Like cabin fever and love sickness, no known medication exists, but it is curable. Right or wrong answers do not apply to your memories. You are in charge this time, you want to save them, and you have the will to work.

No teacher's red pen or editor's blue pencils allowed here. Close the door, take a yellow pad, turn on the computer, or uncover the typewriter. Try a memory exercise like:

☞ The first team I tried out for . . .
☞ All that summer I had a painful crush on . . .
☞ When he fired me, all I felt was shame/anger . . .

You will hear a voice in your ear saying: "That's a good idea," "How old were you?" "What happened next?" "Tell about his quirks," "How did you feel about it?" "How broad were his shoulders?" "Describe the dress you wore."

These exercises and the many others in this book are ice breakers designed to free the narrative of your unique life, which will include the people you have known, and the ordeals, joys, and accomplishments you've had like no other. The emphasis on this workshop in print focuses on personal experience—remembering, feeling it, learning to give it form, meaning, and expression in words.

If you are serious about becoming a writer, you will have to go into training like an athlete with his eye on the Olympics, but it won't hurt as much, and I think you will have more fun writing than jumping over a stick or smashing someone in the face with your fist. In my ongoing workshops, we always start with warm-up exercises, designed to jump-start our imaginations. In the beginning I hear groans, but after a few weeks everyone can write on call as easily as they can pick up a phone. Freeing yourself from looking at a blank sheet of paper and seeing a surrender flag will do great things for your confidence. You learn to write by writing. That's a promise.

Participants often find they can work an exercise into their story. At least, these workouts will enable you to experiment with different types of writing and to deal with a variety of problems ranging from shaping content to controlling tone and discovering your voice. You will create a collection of personal writings revealing your unique inner world of memory, emotion, and imagination. If luck is a lady, you will discover an experience from the past you want to explore and expand.

Try sneaking up on those incidents and people that have shaped your life. See what you can do with one of the following. It could be an insightful path to your past. If it doesn't please you, stash it in your notebook for a while. Maybe you'll come back to it with a clearer picture or a fresh idea. Even the most experienced writer seldom wins the marathon after his first sprint.

Truman Capote wrote three drafts of everything—one on a typewriter—without getting out of bed. The image of this gymnastic feat stumps my imagination, but that is the way he remembered his process. Then he put his third draft away for a week, a month, or even longer before reading or working on it again. Sometimes, even after all that effort, he threw it away. There are still people around, smarting from his caustic portraits, however, who think he did not discard enough.

You, of course, will be discreet, but you might also wad up a few efforts. Some mornings a perverse imp programs our computers for drivel. Don't be discouraged. My mantra, "You learn to write by writing," is true. Just don't discard your memories. They are valuable, a deep mother lode of material no one knows but you.

## WARM-UP EXERCISES

☞ The sounds of whippoorwills, hoot owls, and crickets make me remember . . .

☞ The magic song for us that summer was . . .

☞ Until the end of the conversation, I didn't even realize who he was.

☞ She said she didn't mean to hurt me, but . . .

☞ If only he had not reprimanded me in front of . . .

☞ My mother never approved of . . .

☞ When I was a child, my favorite time of day was . . .

☞ I'll never forget that hotel/meal/plane ride.

☞ The person/place/event in my hometown I remember most . . .

☞ That was the ugliest piece of clothing anyone ever had to wear in front of her friends.

# Chapter 2
# Writing Regularly

*Training is everything. The peach was once a bitter almond; cauliflower is nothing but cabbage with a college education.*

—*Pudd'nhead Wilson*, Mark Twain

Several years ago, I took flying lessons. The first session, in a plane small enough to make me feel as if I had wings, thrilled even this seasoned stewardess. I felt daring, and I loved the perspective. Looking at houses and trees from above turned the world topsy-turvy. I really wanted to learn to fly, but I lived in Chicago and my instructor worked out of a strip in Michigan, two hours away. After a few weeks, I hit a snag in my dissertation. Then a trip to Europe, houseguests, subscription tickets—life intruded.

I began to feel retarded. When I could finally go back to the field, it was like starting all over again. The last time we went up, my instructor, who had begun to sound like a recorded, repetitive message machine, gave me no sympathy. I can still see his square jaw set as if he were gnashing his teeth, hear his gravelly voice saying, "If you want to learn to fly, you *have* to fly regularly."

I've also taken sporadic guitar, clarinet, tennis, and golf lessons. I play none of the above. Then for a time, every boyfriend I had was a bridge player, but since I didn't play between breakups, dummy was my best role. I finally admitted I didn't want to learn to play bridge, so I returned to spending my free time reading literature. I'm better at reading than bridge. I've done it regularly all my life.

You will be delighted to see how much your writing improves if you put in as much time as you did learning to shave or apply mascara.

Several of my students start out saying they only write when inspiration strikes them. If most of us who pay our rent by writing were to follow such a rule, we would soon be homeless. I can picture a *New Yorker* cartoon wherein inspiration is portrayed as a wispy form, like Cathy's ghost in *Wuthering Heights*. She is knocking at my door and I've gone to the movies.

If you are serious about recording the significant events in your life, schedule a regular appointment with your computer, typewriter, or legal pad. Keep it. Writing regularly is one of the few healthy addictions. The light on my computer comes up with the sun and opens with the morning glories. Some of my serious students start at 11:00 P.M. with the moonflowers. Others write on the train to other jobs. One cut her running time in half, exercising her fingers instead. We all write every day. If a universal hour for creativity exists, the news has not yet been announced. Your body chemistry will tell you the time. Not everything you produce will work, but we often have to write through the weeds to find the seeds planted long ago. Exercises can sometimes wake up ideas. Feel free to adapt them to your experience or write from a different perspective. Perhaps one of the following will take you where you want to go:

# JUMP STARTS

☞ I remember tacky souvenirs on a shelf.

☞ I remember the day he didn't come home after work.

☞ I remember feeling stupid.

☞ I remember an eerie glow in the sky.

☞ I remember hoping someone would stop me.

☞ I remember being scared.

☞ I remember eating the berries off the vine.

☞ I remember the sound of the crash.

☞ I remember the buttons.

☞ I remember being repulsed.

☞ I remember thinking I could never be that happy again.

☞ I remember thinking someday she would be sorry.

☞ I remember thinking there was something wrong with him.

# Chapter 3
# Giving Yourself Permission

*And indeed there will be time*
*To wonder "Do I dare?"*

—*"The Love Song of J. Alfred Prufrock,"*
   *T.S. Eliot*

When we were children we were often punished for telling stories. No wonder it's hard to write. How ironic. Here you are landlord to a warehouse crammed with tales eager to be told and no one could know them as you do, but you haven't yet allowed yourself to write them.

When you were a child, did your family have an old car, the kind that "gets" flat tires? Or a sleek sedan with pale blue upholstery where you couldn't eat ice cream? Has anyone ever had to struggle as you did in your first job? Now you realize he was a con artist, but wouldn't anyone have been taken in by his charm?

You have been thinking about those engaging experiences for a long time, maybe telling them too often to people you care about or those who can't escape, like a seatmate on a plane. If your tongue "is the pen of a ready writer," experienced authors say don't talk about your good material, write it. Putting your remembrances on paper could even improve your well-being.

Psychologists and psychiatrists, concerned about people's mental health, usually advise us to tell our stories. They encourage us to take another look at childhood wounds or share middle-age distress. But the urge to follow the good advice is too often impeded by heckling doubt. Why me? My story isn't any more engaging than anyone else's. How could I be so presumptuous?

Barbara Scot parries this concern in the first line of *Prairie Reunion*, a look back at her childhood in Scotch Grove, Iowa: "I offer this personal journey humbly, knowing that your history is as interesting as my own." Scot's memoir reads like a quest, a trip back to the home she remembers as a scene dominated by stern silence and shame. She leaves with a lightened spirit, knowing that having aired the past and visited the ghosts, now at last she can get on with her life.

In *Young Man from the Provinces*, Alan Helms asks why "an anonymous man" would "bother to write a memoir," but the answer lies in his subtitle: "A Gay Life Before Stonewall." Helms says the historians of that milieu have been dying before they could tell their own stories.

If you are still having doubts about writing yours, I can certainly empathize with your hesitancy. Even when I was a kid wanting to ride the rodeo, I knew I would write about my daring adventures. Ironically, I started early, won a couple of minor prizes before intimidation dried my ink and muzzled my muse. Writing required papers on the genius of writers from Shakespeare to Shaw convinced me I had nothing to say. With the help of my writer friend Norma, I gave myself permission about a zillion years too late. Now I feel as if I'll never catch up.

Thank goodness you no longer have to write what the teacher, your mother, the editor, your boss, wants. Assignments are so depressing. Giving yourself permission does not mean being permissive, however. You have to write clear, crisp English sentences and avoid shameless clichés, daft dialogue, and rambling monologues. You will come to know when it's good. Write to please yourself, not someone like the freshman English teacher you probably haven't even seen in years. Let yourself become a part of the story. But here comes another one of those signifying "howevers." Boasting is a bore. Write about yourself with confidence and pleasure. But make sure all the details—people, places, events, anecdotes, ideas, emotions—are moving your story steadily along, taking you where you want to go without bragging, being defensive, or upstaging. In a later chapter, I'll have more to say about how to make the readers see you as the hero of your life without you telling them you are.

Writing about the impressive people and events helps you to make sense of your life. An important reason to write stems from the desire to see if other people have done or felt the same things. It's a test to make one feel normal. All you have to do is convince yourself you are entitled to, which actually seems pretty silly, doesn't it? Getting to where you are hasn't been easy. As the woman in Langston Hughes's poem, "Mother to Son," tells her son, she hasn't climbed through her life on crystal stairs. The steps had tacks and splinters.

Find the negative-voices switch. Turn it off. Slip in a new recording. The vocalist on this CD says:

"You are an engaging person."

"I find your idea interesting. Let's explore it."

"What intriguing experiences you've had, fascinating people you've known."

"Look at what you've accomplished."

"Think about the places you've visited in mind and body."

"You've been a good friend, spouse, parent."

"Too few people know what you've endured, overcome."

"The disappointments and regrets have not defeated you."

"The successes have not spoiled you."

"You have much to be proud of. Use it. You can do it. It's time."

You were born with creative urges. Remember the games of pretend: what if I could fly, what if my dog and I lived in this tree in a jungle, what if I put a worn sheet over the grape arbor and pretended it were a cave in Capri, what if I made a ball gown out of the old drapes? You might still have the poem you wrote when your best friend died from leukemia, a picture of your room with the stars and clouds you painted on the ceiling, notes written in the secret language you and your brother invented, the receipt for peanut butter sandwiches with bananas and raisins you concocted, the triple-decker airplane you carved.

Your ingenious impulses still exist. They are simply being drowned out by the pervasive critics we all acquire along the way. Our judges tend to operate on a high, usually shrill, frequency.

An old crone with a nasty voice ladling out doubt and self-loathing is a composite of all those disapproving, nagging comments and reactions you've been hoarding since you first heard:

"Don't"

"Unacceptable"

"Ridiculous"

"Rejected"

"Fired"

"Dismissed"

"You're ugly and your mother dresses you funny"

"You've disappointed, embarrassed, shamed me/the family/the community/the company/your country"

"You can't play on our team"

"You're not allowed"

"You weren't invited"

"That's not right"

"What will the neighbors think?"

"We don't do it that way here"

"Not what I had in mind"

"Who do you think you are?"

You could probably even find some dynamite material behind some of the harpy's sticks and stones.

Don't think for a moment you have dibs on this disparaging hag. In this regard you are not unique. The spoiler operates ubiquitously. Laurence Olivier and Lily Pons threw up before each dazzling performance. Impossible as it seems, Jane Austen hid what she wrote from her family and friends. Barbra Streisand and Carly Simon are so plagued by stage fright, they cannot face performing as often as their fans would buy tickets. An orchestra conductor swore on his honor a well-known opera diva was so terrified onstage, at first, that her eyes crossed and she couldn't follow his direction.

Disentangle yourself from the ghosts. Stockpiling those disparaging memories defeats and hurts you. Besides, they take up too much room. I'll tell you a secret. Contrary voices suffer from middle-age spread. The longer you keep them, the more they swell to become bigger and uglier until they consume all the storage space in your head, crowding out not only your creative instincts but, worse, the confidence to expose your singular voice and view. Fortunately, they shrivel and shrink in the light. Try it. The first to wilt is the person who said you'd never be worth a damn.

When you earn enough money to buy a car, you feel entitled to own it, to use it as you wish. How could you not feel authorized to write the stories of your life? Think what you have paid for those experiences. I promise to pester you into believing in the validity of your lives as grist for absorbing stories.

Look at the fame Proust received for writing about a cup of tea and a bit of cake, for Pete's sake. As an adult, analyzing a feeling of great joy over his tea sent him back to his childhood in Combray. He says, "It is plain that the object of my quest, the truth, lies not in the cup but in myself. . . ."

After being shot down over Bosnia, Air Force Captain Scott O'Grady's quest was to stay alive. When he was rescued, he wrote (with Jeff Coplon) *Return With Honor*, a memoir about his grueling six days of eating leaves and ants, and avoiding land mines and being captured. Coplon says it used to be pretty hard for him to get a date, but on the promotional tour for his book, many women proposed to him. I can't promise giving yourself consent to write your story will improve your love life, but hey, it has happened.

Don't think you have to eat insects or be shot out of an airplane to have a story to tell, and don't be intimidated by Proust's quest, which went on for volumes and volumes. You can begin with a small bite. Try one of the following exercises.

Permission granted.

## LIBERATORS

☞ Even after all this time, I still expect to hear . . . tishing, tishing in the background when I . . .

☞ After I got the job/received the promotion/gained recognition, I wanted to go back to . . . to tell him, "I told you so."

☞ Surely no one becomes a bad parent on purpose or intends to make an offspring's life more difficult. That's why I always wonder why my mother/father . . .

☞ When I'm pleased with what I see in the mirror, I only wish . . . could see me now.

☞ Today it seems inconsequential, but at the time I thought I would die of humiliation.

☞ For a long time I thought when I lost my job/spouse/lover I had lost my identity.

☞ . . . believed in me from the beginning.

☞ He was the type of person who could only feel important by making others feel unimportant.

☞ Fortunately, she wasn't the only beauty in the world.

☞ Now I realize the beast was stuffed with straw.

☞ Today I know we grant people permission to intimidate us, but I did not know it then.

# Chapter 4
# Thinking Like a Writer

*Where is the love, beauty,*
*and truth we seek,*
*But in our mind?*

—*"Julian and Maddalo,"*
  *Percy Bysshe Shelley*

Writers don't wear a badge or all have gray eyes, but you can always recognize one. He notices what you're wearing, what you say, the way you move and sit, the mole just below your left ear. *Everything is material.* Most are discreet, but don't be alarmed if he whips out a notebook on the spot to write down one of your interesting remarks. If you are serious about putting your memories into words, you will begin to behave in the same bizarre manner. Writers are scavengers, always scrounging for language and images to illuminate their work. One of my fondest memories involves a woman who was a master at not missing a trick, a plot, or a character.

Norma was the first person I knew well who wrote "writer" under occupation on her IRS form. When we met, I was a University of Chicago teacher who occasionally wrote about other people's work. When an article appeared praising one of her books, she asked me to have lunch when I came to New York. We talked for four hours and only stopped when the waiters threw us out to prepare for the dinner crowd. A few blocks away, I realized I had left an umbrella at the restaurant. After a quick dash to retrieve it, I found Norma walking slowly with her head bowed. I spoke to her, but this woman who had just asked—and I had told her—my bank balance, my political preference, when I lost my virginity, didn't recognize me. A few months later, I would understand she had already been plotting a novel about a midwestern woman who taught at a university noted for rigor, but who really wanted to be a writer. The protagonist had short curly hair, a penchant for blue, and wore lily of the valley perfume. Norma, this woman who thought like a writer even in her dreams, had plagiarized my life.

Though bits and pieces of me continued to appear in her work, I forgave Norma because I learned so much from simply observing how she thought, worked, and discovered her ideas in the world around her and in everything from classic myths to lonely hearts columns. My students are not always as forgiving. Recently Tom said my books encouraging people to think like a writer should come with a warning label like those found on cigarette packs. He is a successful corporate lawyer, has a cushy job with a Mercedes for a company car, travels internationally, and has a salary rich enough to rent a penthouse apartment. "Sounds terrific," I said as he listed the perks. "It is . . . if you want to be a lawyer," this sensitive young man, who has come to think like a writer, replied.

Maria, on her way to work, missed her subway stop when she became intrigued with the rhythm and figures of speech in two dockworkers' conversation. A woman at the library thought Chip was getting fresh as he leaned too close, when he was only trying to decide how to describe the delightful fragrance she was wearing.

On her deathbed Pat Conroy's mother said, "Son, I find it hard to relax while I'm dying, knowing you're going to write down every damn word I say," and he did in his novel *Beach Music.*

Be prepared. You'll see a woman wearing a hat that reminds you of the one your first piano teacher wore, and
probably walk off the curb trying to find the details to de-
pict the atrocity Miss Parker wore to introduce you at the
recital where you forgot your part in the concerto. If the
man sitting next to you on the plane twists his hair just
as the most insecure boss you ever had did, it's probably
not a good idea to ask him to do it again while you take
notes.

Granted, thinking like a writer on the job can be hazard-
ous to your future Social Security checks if you are an
airline controller, trade options, or throw hot rivets at tall
buildings, but in most cases it's a sure cure for boredom.
Writers notice things like seagull's evil eyes, how mice who
squeeze into a drawer couldn't have any bones. They smell
the rosewater on their grandmother's hands, the odor of
old, briny grease where too many onions have sizzled. They
hear the wail and whine of a tired engine begging for
mercy; the pure, high note from a triumphant street trum-
peter working Madison Avenue, but playing for the gods.

Thinking like a writer is like getting new glasses with a
stronger prescription. You could see before, but your world
seemed fuzzy, a tad out of focus. Now things appear
brighter, clearer, sharper, more interesting, and they make
more sense.

Walking through the world with your senses alert sharp-
ens your ability to recapture your personal past, the slip-
pery heritage of your experience. When these
remembrances emerge in the present for a brief moment,
put them on paper before they again withdraw into the
recess of memory. Alienation from memories dooms people
to live in a constant present, cut off from the past and
the future.

See if any of the following suggestions can dredge up
something forgotten:

# THINKING LIKE A WRITER

☞ The snowsuit felt like . . .

☞ Diving into the water where we weren't supposed to swim . . .

☞ I earned the money mowing lawns and spent it all on . . .

☞ After the deed was done and she had cut my hair, I . . .

☞ For lunch on Saturday, we always had fried egg sandwiches slathered with mayonnaise.

☞ When I had the measles, my spots were bigger and brighter than anyone else's.

☞ The first year we were married, we couldn't afford to go to restaurants, so we . . .

☞ The rake raised blisters on my fingers that felt like . . .

☞ My first office smelled like . . .

☞ I wore it because I thought it looked beautiful, but it was the most uncomfortable . . .

☞ I had my first chocolate soda at . . .

☞ I worked for an unbridled bully.

☞ A beaded evening bag

☞ My first tie

☞ A broken bone

☞ The first divorce in our family

☞ A secret place

☞ The lilac bush

# Chapter 5
# Keeping a Notebook

Look sharply after your thoughts.
They come unlooked for, like a
new bird seen on your trees, and, if
you turn to your usual task,
disappear . . .

—Ralph Waldo Emerson

Writer and composer Paul Bowles thought of the title for his novel *The Sheltering Sky* while riding down Fifth Avenue on the top of a double-decker New York bus. He wrote it in the small notebook he always carried. The title for Sartre's play *No Exit* also began in Bowles's notebook when he saw the sign on a subway car, wrote it down, and took it home to his friend. Perish the thought if Bowles had not carried his notebook. The ideal title that has become a universal metaphor could have been lost. Sartre and the world could have been stuck with something like *Eternal Suffering* or *Penance Without End.*

Dawn Powell, a fine and important writer adored by a few lucky readers, died in 1965, but keeps being rediscovered. Recently her novel *My Home Is Far Away* and her diaries were reissued. The diaries kept from 1931 to 1965 do not record earthshaking events, but are a writer's notebook filled with raw material she would later use in her novels, as you will use what you collect in your memoir. In one entry she wrote: " 'Satire' is the technical word for writing of people as they are; 'romantic,' the other extreme of people as they are to themselves—but both of these are the truth." Powell's notebooks show she believed in love, even though she knew better.

Don't despair if you have not been recording your revealing thoughts and observations for thirty-four years. You have your memories, but I suggest you start the notebook immediately for those days when your brain seems to have taken a holiday.

Joan Didion says she keeps a notebook for the mornings when the world seems drained of wonder and she is only going through the motions of writing. On those bankrupt mornings she tells herself a forgotten entry will be waiting, paid passage back to the world out there. If not, it's a way of keeping in touch with her memories, like her finding a recipe for sauerkraut tucked into a memory of a frightening storm. "It all comes back. . . . I was on Fire Island when I first made that sauerkraut, and it was raining, and we drank a lot of bourbon and ate the sauerkraut and went to bed . . . and I felt safe."

Anne Morrow Lindbergh's *Gifts from the Sea* began as thoughts stashed in a notebook. In the introduction she says:

> I began these pages for myself, in order to think out my own particular pattern of living, my own individual balance of life, work, and human relationships. And since I think best with a pencil in my hand, I started naturally to write. I had the feeling, when the thoughts first clarified on paper, that my experience was very different from other people's. [Are we all under this illusion?]

For one who wants to stay in touch, one who thinks best with a pencil in hand, one who thinks like a writer, keeping a notebook handy is as essential as writing regularly. You think you will remember that good idea, a clever quip, the guy whose many chins lay neatly folded above his collar like Cousin Raymond's, but you hardly ever do.

When I go to bed, I turn into a stone until morning, but many people keep a pad on the bedside table. This is a good idea not only for insomniacs, but for those who in the morning can resist the first cup of coffee long enough to spend the first few minutes reviewing dreams or capturing fresh ideas for their stories. Some resourceful writers put a thermos of coffee by their notebooks before they go to sleep.

Motivated by a tinge of recollection, men might long for the days when Victorian writers like Dickens thought great thoughts while their morning tea was being served in bed, but I assume the remembrance of such service surfaces less frequently from the collective unconscious of women. I doubt Emily Brontë or Jane Austen ever had that luxury.

Students ask what kind of notebook to buy. *Handy* is the operative word. Whatever fits in your pocket, briefcase, or purse works best. After being intimidated by leather-bound gifts with gilded edges, I've learned to look for the least luxurious. Who could dare to write, "Hey, sucker," or misspell a word in a book from Tiffany's? Mine are spirals with several divisions like a portable filing cabinet.

Titles can suggest topics. Look at *The New Yorker*'s "Talk of the Town" and try not to think of something you could write. Remember the "Hers" column in *The New York Times*? I always thought of it as "Mine." Too bad Ruth Prawer Jhabvala has already called her novel *Shards of Memory*. It would make a dynamite name for a memoir. Keep a section in your notebook for possible titles and epithets that might motivate you.

From the reader's point of view it is interesting to read someone else's memories not only for a different perspective on the human condition, but for the pleasure of how the events, people, places, and times jog their own recollections. Mention buggies and my mother could tell fascinating tales about fast horses, wild boys, manhood-testing races, lost wheels, broken axles, and courting practices that didn't seem quaint to her. My sister was pursued by a young man in a sleek, low-slung Corvette that kept up with the wind, or so my father said. Pickup trucks and motorcycles painted with fire-eating symbols seemed to impress the women of my nephew's generation at the University of Iowa. Mention Checker cabs or the A train and a

New Yorker can talk forever. In Chicago it was the el.
Rumor has it that in California there's a car for each mem-
ber of the family, even the cat, but everyone from San
Francisco seems to remember at least one experience on
BART. DC-7s do it for me.

I suggest you reserve one section of your notebook for
nostalgic "trigger words and phrases" like the following.
Add your own.

| | |
|---|---|
| Cadillac with fins | bell-bottoms |
| love beads | junk bonds |
| WPA art | hula hoop |
| VJ Day | Ted Williams |
| David and Chet | Sirhan Sirhan |
| the Beatles | "I have a dream" |
| ration books | jitterbug, bunny hop, frug |
| Black October | mimeograph machine |
| Strawberry Fields | "White Christmas" |
| the Brooklyn Dodgers | B Altman's |
| Blackstone Rangers | Prohibition |
| the Cold War | Geraldine Ferraro |
| the good black dress | Eagle Scout |
| saddle shoes | rolltop desk |
| vaccinations | Scarlett O'Hara |
| Fala, Checkers, Socks | the Chicago Seven |
| Lester Lannon | *Collier's* |
| Conveyors | the Hit Parade |
| nylons | garter belts |
| Tian An Men Square | ducktail |
| jelly bread | Judy Garland |

"Ask not what your country can do . . ."

Collect words whose sound or image taps your imagination. Z words like *zoom, zip, zing, zilch, zap, zealot, zither,
zonked,* tickle the tongue. Remember how you liked to say,
"Flopsy, Mopsy, Cottontail, and Peter" when you were a
child? "Rubbish" is an expressive word. I use it often when
listening to political speeches. Police have turned *perpetrator*—a bad choice from the beginning—into a cliché. Try to
picture a perpetrator. *Crook* with all its implications
works better.

A man usually tells more than he intends when he calls a woman: *lady, chick, bird, broad, bitch, dame, gal, babe.*

Keep a section for observations and stolen bits of dialogue. Strangers on the street, as well as our family and friends, do and say things to reveal character unaware. Copy it down. You might be able to use it. Recently I passed a middle-aged couple just as she was saying, "Honey, you not only abuse me . . .".

My husband's aunt, a school principal, convinced me she was a lady when I noticed she wore silk stockings to vacuum the rug.

I am still not certain if it was the strength of his personality or his creativity that caused my father's made-up words to become a part of our family vocabulary. When the weather turned cold, he said it was "crimpy." Looking at my baby sister for the first time, he said, "Now, she's a dilly." Years later when Dairy Queen began to advertise Dilly Bars, I felt they should have paid him a residual.

After having lunch with a woman whose fortune had come lately, I suggested a subway would be our fastest means of transportation. "I'm too old and too rich to ride the trains," she replied.

I once had an appointed secretary I couldn't fire who enhanced her thin hair with a fake glob of curls she stuck on top of her head with the aid of an attached comb. When Marge got angry at me, students, the system—which was often—she used her head to hammer home her wrathful words. Invariably the clump of phony hair sailed away, landing at her feet like a flattened rat. Marge landed in my notebook.

Doing research for her book *In the Cut,* Suzanna Moore became obsessed by talk in the subway, where she learned things like "freezerator" for refrigerator, "knockin' boots" for sexual intercourse, "gangsters" for breasts. Moore says writers always are—or should be—watching, listening.

Good writers change our perspective often about the simplest everyday things, like fog coming "on little cat's feet," suggesting "good fences make good neighbors," comparing a fast life to a candle—"my candle burns at both ends."

The following are notebook exercises you might be able to draw from when you are ready to write your memoir:

# NOTEBOOK EXERCISES

☞   Make a list of words that make you laugh.

☞   Make a list of words that make you hungry.

☞   Make a list of words like *rush* or *rumble* whose sound implies the action.

☞   Make a list of sad words.

☞   Make a list of frightening words.

☞   Make a list of words that suggest elegance.

☞   Make a list of words that suggest beauty.

☞   Make a list of the most memorable people you have known.

☞   Make a list of song titles popular when you were young.

☞   Make a list of movies or stars that were your favorites as a teenager.

☞   Make a list of all the automobile accidents you have endured.

☞   Make a list of shades of nail polish and lipstick you've worn.

☞   Make a list of products you only wish you could still buy.

☞   Make two lists of vacations—the best and the worst.

☞   Make a list of your annual salary as far back as you can remember.

☞   Make a list of things that still shock you.

☞   Make a list of ways your ancestors earned a living.

☞   Describe the different places your mail has been delivered.

☞   Describe the best real estate investment you ever made.

☞   Describe the most magnificent maneuver you've ever seen made on a playing field.

☞   Describe a friend or family member's unusual habits or gestures.

☞ Describe a strange costume a friend or family member wears.

☞ Describe the screwiest defense anyone has ever offered you for bad behavior.

☞ Describe your case of unrequited love.

☞ Write down interesting, character-revealing, or wacky conversations you've overheard.

☞ What would be an interesting comparison for the following?:

your hungry cat
your closet
your son's closet
your stockbroker's sales pitch
the basement in your house
the sound of your boss's angry voice
telemarketing at dinnertime
the lonely woman in the park
the cousin you can't stand
the man you didn't marry
an asthma attack
a backache
walking barefoot in morning dew
breaking waves
Monday night football
takeoff
alimony

# Chapter 6
# Achieving Distance

*"Not Waving but Drowning"*

—*Stevie Smith*

Truman Capote isn't the only person who had eccentric relatives, and not only Russell Baker grew up poor. The story Tennessee Williams tells about his sister's lobotomy breaks your heart, but your family hasn't escaped pain. So Willie Morris's dog Skip played football and could (sort of) drive a car. What about your cat, a lady who has had a shady past? Pete Hammill made a ton of money admitting he had once been a drunk, Richard Rayner confesses at Cambridge he learned to be a crook, and Michael Ryan published a memoir the reviewer called "the portrait of an artist as a young pervert," for pity's sake.

Finding material among your memories will not be a problem; selecting could be. If your divorce is raging in the courts and in your mind, as tempting as it may be to tell your side, it's best not to choose it as a topic for your memoir. You will write about it, of course, but not while you are in the middle of it. Now your perspective is too narrow, too emotionally clouded, and you remember too many details that will eventually not seem as important. Impossible as it might feel now, after you settle the splitting of the silver and the photographs, you might even come to see some humor in the argument over the sugar tongs, Aunt Harriet's wedding gift, especially since neither of you has ever owned a box of cubed sugar or could abide Aunt Harriet.

Time has a profound effect on our emotions, understanding, and writing style. Think about the day you were in a car accident. How would you have expressed your feelings seconds after impact, and how would you tell it now? At the moment we receive a phone call saying someone we love has died, we can't imagine ever leading a sane life again. I hung up on my sister when she tried to tell me Mother was dead. I didn't want to hear that. But eventually I called her back and now we are beginning to look at the gifts our mother left us, memories that have influenced who we are.

Achieving distance helps us to comprehend not only what has happened, but why it has occurred and what it means to us. Mark Twain said he was amazed at how much his father had learned by the time Mark was twenty-one. In college, I remember reading his remark and feeling sheepish.

At college age, when I was still trying on identities, Che Guevara appealed to the rebel in me. Thirty years later when his diaries, written when he was twenty-three, were published in English, I agreed with the reviewer who said it was impossible to read his words and not weep for Che Guevara, who had a noble soul, but died before he had attained enough distance and experience to be able to see what would happen to the great Communist future in Cuba.

Nigerian freedom fighter and writer Ken Saro-Wiwa wrote his first memoir, *On a Darkling Plain*, about the Biafran Civil War, but as with Che Guevara, he was only able to leave a diary about the final struggle between the Ogoni tribe, of which he was a member, and the Royal Dutch/Shell group. Just days before he was executed, his son got a computer disk to London detailing Saro-Wiwa's detention by the Nigerian government and the conflict between his tribe and the oil company. He ended the account with references to other hardships endured by his tribe: "But that's another story, if I live to tell the tale."

It hurts too bad to think about the reflective book we will never read by this fine writer and brave man.

I no longer recall who, but someone convincing told me to let experiences lie for seven years before trying to understand their significance. Liquor and memories are among the few things that improve with aging.

Take a walk through your house. You will find memories ready to be told tucked in every corner, tacked on every wall, hung in every closet. There is a souvenir from that ghastly ski trip when the first day someone stole your traveler's checks and the second day you broke your ankle. My hatbox contains enough material for a lifetime of work. I kept my stew cap designed by Raymond Lowey because everyone said I looked good in it. I wish he had designed something reasonable for academics to wear with their robes. I scare small children in this thing that looks like a pincushion with the stuffing taken out. There's the chic, confidence-building black derby I wore on auspicious occasions in the seventies when many of us were testing the water as the first women corporate executives. One of my students recently gave me a ball cap like the one I used to wear to play softball . . . not very well. I always felt like Scarlett O'Hara in that picture hat. The fez looked better in Tangier, but I still sometimes wear the French beret.

Open your jewelry box and let the memories out.

Shame, regret, and jealousy, the powerful emotions that eat us alive, have less bite on a sheet of paper.

Untie the blue ribbon on that stack of letters.

Look at your Christmas card list. The names scratched through might be the most engrossing. Do you remember why you were angry at Henry? Do you still not know why Alice stopped sending you a holiday greeting? And Mark? Where do you suppose that rascal calls home these days?

If you haven't noticed the stories lurking in the family photograph album, you haven't been paying attention. Rogues and eccentrics clamor for attention, and their stories are easier and more fun to tell. I once had a gentleman caller who continually said his father was a saint. The man in question had been dead for fifteen years, which made it easier for him to maintain his reputation, and my friend, who was a persuasive writer, never tried to put a proving portrait on paper. Saints' stories read better in the church liturgy, and if it's a self-portrait, forget it.

The following are suggestions to help you recall the saints and sinners in your life and to recover elements of lost time. Amend, add to, change them until they work for you. How long you have been walking these paths makes a difference, of course, but to people who've voted in many national elections, seven years is the recent past.

## THE RECENT PAST

- ☞ The first time I saw the man/woman I will marry.
- ☞ It wasn't even my fight, but the unfairness of the situation sucked me into it.
- ☞ He/she was impossible to please.
- ☞ He was a liar. I couldn't trust him. Unfortunately, I loved him.
- ☞ Once I sold myself to the devil and he sent . . .
- ☞ Someone forced me to lie to save your face or his.
- ☞ A dream I have never forgotten.
- ☞ A vacation directed by the gods who like to joke around.
- ☞ It was impossible to please both of them.
- ☞ I didn't even mean to have an affair. It just happened.
- ☞ A coincidence changed my life.
- ☞ When I signed the papers I was so scared, my hands shook and my signature was wavy.
- ☞ The truth embarrassed me, so I fudged it.
- ☞ The message on the answering machine splattered me like an elephant gun.
- ☞ I had done little thinking about, and less planning for, retirement, and then suddenly the time had snuck up on me.
- ☞ Changing where I lived changed my life.
- ☞ My boss called it outplacement. I called it being put out to pasture.
- ☞ I wasn't guilty, but I couldn't prove my innocence to her.
- ☞ At the time, I thought about jumping in front of a train.
- ☞ At the time, I thought I couldn't lose.
- ☞ At the time, I thought it was only a stopover.

# Chapter 7
# Childhood Memories

*I like very much people telling me
about their childhood, but they'll
have to be quick or else I'll be telling
them about mine.*

—*"Reminiscences of Childhood,"*
*Dylan Thomas*

Remembering childhood is as natural as rain and certainly not childish. We go back because those were delightful years filled with fun, or we try to ease the pain that hasn't gone away. Looking back across the years adds another hue like a sepia-toned photograph, giving us a second life or a second chance.

Innumerable fine writers have gone back for another look at what they experienced as children, and called it fiction. You can call yours memories.

Dickens touched our hearts, raised our awareness, and changed child labor laws with David Copperfield's trials, which were loosely based on the impoverished life Dickens led when his father was in Marshalsea, England's debtors' prison. In *Little Dorrit* he returns for another look at the effect Marshalsea had on poor children's lives, and still had hundreds of pages of pithy things to say. One wonders if Oliver Twist's last name isn't a pun when you read another account of youthful Dickens's pauper life—this time with only the slight twist of Oliver's being a child of unknown parentage.

Mark Twain earned his reputation as the Father of American Literature with his major contributions, *The Adventures of Tom Sawyer* and *The Adventures of Huckleberry Finn*. The novels are two creative versions of his boyhood life on the Mississippi River. Critics contend Twain split himself in half to create the two boys: Tom, the boastful, impractical romantic, and Huck, the kindhearted pragmatist. Most of the other characters, even Pap, can be identified with untransformed Hannibal, Missouri, residents. Only their names have been changed.

The people in the villages on the Illinois side of the Mississippi where I grew up more than a hundred years later had not changed that much. I was a consultant to the Mark Twain Library in Berkeley, California, for a couple of years. A thousand miles away, reading Twain's accounts of Hannibal eccentrics, I began to think of Shobonier, Illinois, population five hundred, where, in spite of parental threats and pleas, all of us kids hung out at Rose Hailey's and ate her cornbread. Superstitious, illiterate Rose, who had an open sore on her neck and could have stood a good scrub, smoked a corncob pipe, wore a sunbonnet and high-button shoes you couldn't buy anymore, and told us preposterous stories. If we laughed, she chased us home with her broom. We speculated her son Harrison, who could ride a bicycle slower than a worm could crawl, was about a hundred, which had to make Rose older than Methuselah. When we asked her, she always told us she was born in green bean time, so figure it out for ourselves.

Twain's Pap and my Rose Hailey probably aren't any more bizarre than some of those who added color to your childhood.

Faulkner said until Hemingway wrote *The Old Man and The Sea*, he had shaped his characters out of his own clay. I'm not certain the old man is not also Hemingway fighting to regain his reputation, which had slipped with the critics, but certainly the Nick Adams stories could have come straight out of the diary accounts of hunting and fishing trips young Ernest took with his father, who finally taught him not only how to hunt and to fish, but how to end life's pain through suicide.

Years after he returns from World War II, John Knowles's character Gene goes back to his (Knowles's and Gene's) prep school to face the fear he had lived with for fifteen years and finally make "a separate peace."

Dorothy Allison's horrific story *Bastard Out of Carolina* received deserved praise as a novel, but reading it, I also felt as if I were watching and listening as the author lanced a boil swollen with the memories of her own childhood. She and her character Bone had experienced poverty, contempt from the self-righteous community, and sexual abuse by members of their own family. Told without malice, Allison wrote about Bone's fury and her finding forgiveness. Later, in her memoir, *Two or Three Things I Know for Sure*, the author confirmed she had shared both experiences.

Poets often find subjects stashed away, like their toys and christening robes, in childhoods not much different from yours. May Swenson's "The Centaur" strikes a familiar chord: "The summer that I was ten—/Can it be there was only one/summer that I was ten? . . ."

One of my favorite versions of childhood memories is Dylan Thomas's charming *A Child's Christmas in Wales*: "I made a snowman and my brother knocked it down and I knocked him down and then we had tea."

Once a history professor, implying truth could only be found in his discipline, told me history was what happened and literature was how we felt about what had happened. It's a tidy definition, until one considers point of view. Compare a northern and a southern historian's view of the Civil War, or Canadian history told from the viewpoint of one from French ancestry and another from English descent. No one can tell your history but you; not even a member of your family will see it as you have, and perish the thought if an antagonist were to tell it from her perspective.

My sister and I are exactly the same height, both have curly hair. We drew from the same gene pool, and still agree that blue jeans have been the best invention in the past two hundred years. Fortunately, we were loved children, wanted by both parents, but the similarities stop there. We had very different childhoods, very different parents. I am thirteen years older. My mother and father were young, feisty, energetic, just starting out. Hers were comfortably established, approaching middle age, mellowed and more prudent. Mine took me to the horse races when I was two weeks old. The first person I raced on horseback was my mother. Daddy swam the flooding river with me on his back and danced with me in a roadhouse that had a questionable reputation. My sister had baby-sitters, learned to swim in a pool, had a cocker spaniel, not a horse, for a pet. Do our childhoods explain why I wanted to fly and my sister wanted to get married and have children, why I still drive too fast and she has a cold fear of highway patrolmen? I don't know, but I find digging speculatively into our pasts fascinating. I think you will find yours enticing too.

To open the door to that storehouse where you packed away your childhood, see if any of the following hold a key:

## CHILDHOOD MEMORIES

☞ The biggest bully a kid ever had to face.

☞ Winter viewed through the window of my childhood bedroom was . . .

☞ The first money I ever earned.

☞ The worst Christmas.

☞ The day I learned to ride a bike/Rollerblades.

☞ My best friend in third grade.

☞ The teacher I still remember for good or ill.

☞ The dog, cat, horse, I still wish I had.

☞ To this day I still haven't told anyone what really happened.

☞ It hurt worse than a whipping.

☞ We were too polite to call him the village idiot. We just said he was touched.

☞ We worried a great deal about what the neighbors would think.

☞ Some things you never get over. I can still cry about . . .

☞ I've never again been as proud of an accomplishment as I was when . . .

☞ The problem I caused between my mother and father was intentional/unintentional.

☞ My first time on the stage was a . . .

☞ What I liked best about the dime store in my hometown . . .

☞ All the other kids had . . .

☞ My secret hideout.

☞ My childhood persona.

☞ My worst moral decision.

# Chapter 8
# Families by Birth and Marriage

*Happy families are all alike; every unhappy family is unhappy in its own way.*

—Anna Karenina,
  *Leo Nikolayevich Tolstoy*

I doubt anyone has ever lived who did not at some point wonder, especially during adolescence, if she had been adopted. Usually after a good night's sleep, the idea fades away with her bad dreams. We might wish our families had had the good taste to settle in a more picturesque place, provide spiffier ancestors, acquire more money, education, or sophistication, but given the option to change places, most of us would not.

Whether your mission has been to live up to, or to overcome, your lineage, a multitude of memories ripened on your family tree. You remember the rivalries, expectations, disappointments, and attempts to control, as well as the fun and the love. We all had relatives who embarrassed and exasperated us, as well as those who made us proud.

No one sees those relatives as we do, especially not spouses. When I read Joan Didion's essay "On Going

Home," I felt as if she had plagiarized my memories. It was *my* husband who objected to my calling home, not where we lived, but where my parents did. It was my husband who said I fell back into my family's ways as soon as I opened the door. It was my husband who said we only talked about people in mental hospitals or booked on drunk-driving charges, or fretted about the price of land per acre.

If you have been married, you have going-home stories to write.

No matter how old we are, when our mothers and fathers die, we feel like orphans. In retrospect, it seems as if I were born knowing sometime I would have to give up Mother, as if good things couldn't last. But my strong, stubborn father? He was immortal. When our plane landed in Paris on an appropriately wet, gloomy December morning and I learned he had died before his time, I was furious. As my husband and I sat in the yellow light of Notre Dame Cathedral waiting for the next flight back to Illinois, I felt betrayed. Silently, my solid, dependable father had promised to see me through. I had been cheated. All this time I had felt as if I were a free spirit, flying high. Hitting with a thud the French soil which hadn't seemed so foreign before, I was suddenly afraid my father had been holding my kite string, firmly.

The pain or the anger caused by the death of family members, especially parents, has driven many poets to strive for words to express their anguish. At first, Sylvia Plath's lines from "Daddy"—about having to kill him, but feeling regret that he died before she could, shocked her critics. After her own death by suicide, the poem added evidence to the depth of her despair. Dylan Thomas's advice to his dying father has become a rallying cry: "Do not go gentle into that good night."

With a few exceptions, like Gore Vidal, who banished his mother from his life twenty years before her death and did not attend her funeral, most people feel they do not have long enough to come to know and understand their parents, even when they survive into old age. It has to be torturous for kids whose parents die early, especially for children of the famous like Martin Luther King, John and Bobby Kennedy, when hundreds of thousands of people seem to have known their progenitors and expect the children to live up to someone they barely remember.

Humphrey Bogart's son Stephen, eight years old when his father died, grappled unsuccessfully with the famous-father problem for years. Finally he faced it by writing *Bogart*, a poignant and painfully raw memoir. The book was a son's search to fill in his hazy memories and to understand the public and personal sides of a man he scarcely knew. Stephen also wrote a novel, *Play It Again*, which was published at the same time. The novel, whose title refers to a famous line from the Bogey film *Casablanca*, blurs the line between memoir and fiction. The fabricated detective is the son of a tough-guy movie star who died when the hero was a boy, and an aging grande-dame movie star—who is the murder victim. Reviewer Caryn James said, "Of course, it's fiction, but it's fair to say . . . Bogart [Stephen] kills off his mom, then lets his alter ego forgive her for years of emotional neglect. Except for the murder, it sounds a lot like his life."

Don't be discouraged because Bogart's books were published although they were "unremarkable in literary terms," according to critic Caryn James. Of course, it helps to have famous parents to get your story into print, but there are other rewards for writing a memoir. As Anne Lamott said in *bird by bird*, publishing is not what it's cracked up to be, but writing is. If you write about the relationship between you and your mother or father, you will be amazed how much you learn about both of you, and that's another promise.

Seeing Isaac Bashevis Singer from his son, Israel Zamir's, perspective in his memoir, *Journey to My Father, Isaac Bashevis Singer*, diminishes the famous man if not his work. Zamir was five when Singer left his Communist wife Ronia, who had been imprisoned in Poland for her views. Mother and son finally found safety in Palestine, while Singer settled in New York, but wrote promising letters about reconciliation. Because he forgot to mention that after five years he had married Alma Wasserman, Ronia did not remarry for twelve years. After twenty years, when Zamir visited him, Singer said, "My stories are my children. . . . Children are a burden. . . . Don't get me wrong, I'm loyal to you as every father is to his son. But

on condition that nothing gets in the way of my writing."
When Zamir, who had done Hebrew translations of his father's work, proudly showed the first published volume of
his own stories to Singer, he said, "Why don't you translate
my books instead of writing your own?"

British poet Blake Morrison's *And When Did You Last
See Your Father*, a memoir about a testy relationship with
his dad, a Yorkshire doctor who wanted his son to follow
him in the profession, is another case in point. In the beginning Dr. Morrison appears through his son's childhood
recollections to be an overbearing cad, an arrogant cheap-
skate who will do anything to get his way. But the reader
begins to change her opinion as the adult son comes to
appreciate the older man's quirkiness.

I thought Jay Parini's review might be a motivator for any
of you attempting to make something of your memories:

> On one level, this is a book about how a bright boy with
> literary aspirations gradually learns how to withstand his
> father's blandishments without losing affection for him. But
> it is also a book about confronting the loss of one's own
> childhood in the death of a parent. So much vanishes, so
> quickly, and one can do nothing about it.

Libraries abound with memoirs focusing on relationships
with fathers, progeny trying to bring order and understanding to their fathers' powerful presence on the chaotic
or painful route to their maturity. My father has tried his
best to take over this book. Sometimes I think he is paying
me back for my innocent indiscretions as a child:

Mother and I went to town to the movies every time the
bill changed. My father couldn't understand why we would
spend good money to cry or be scared out of our wits. Once
for about a week, after a film in which Peter Lorre strangled
all the women with his long white scarf, I demanded to
sleep with Mother. Drapes hanging from a pole had replaced the French doors originally opening to my room. In
the dark, those drapes looked just like the white scarf. I
went back to my room when my father threatened no more
movies. Our bedrooms were back to back. I still knocked
on the wall to ask them what was so funny. After I started
to school, my father came home for lunch often.

Whatever my father's motivation, like the ghost of Hamlet's father's, Daddy is still at it, making me feel I must earn his love. But I'm on to him. Oh, he probably will coerce me into making him the focal point of my memories. Some things you never get over. But I'll smile this time. At thirteen I didn't find my gnawing need to win his approval very funny.

Keeping my father off every page has been like trying to stuff an air bag back into its container. I suggest you say "I remember" and listen to your stories that want to be told. You might not have dramatic epiphanies, but with a little luck you could fit more pieces into the jigsaw puzzle of your life.

Author Walter Edmond's memoir, *Tales My Father Never Told*, is a collection of essays about a boy and a difficult, narcissistic father. Edmond also says that his father had been sent to an all-girl's school as a child, and had been forced to wear girl's clothes to be less conspicuous. He determines his father had become a tyrant out of fear he would not measure up as a man. Armed with this insight, Edmond concludes they had actually loved each other—a disclosure that he says might be justification enough for "this small book."

I can't promise writing yours will allow you to penetrate all the family mysteries, but I wager you, too, will discover enough to justify having done it. Sometimes the process leads you back to where you started.

Alan Helms, fueled by grasshoppers from the Astor Bar, actually cartwheeled through Times Square when he came from Indiana, where the message had seemed to a young, handsome, gay man that life was "hard & mean & unyielding, unlovely & without grace. . . ." In his honest memoir *Young Man from the Provinces: A Gay Life Before Stonewall*, he told how he used his assets—especially his looks and sexual preference—to land a part in Noel Coward's play *Sail Away*, and how his hopeful nobody of a mother drove from bleak Indiana to share his opening night. After the show he left her standing on the sidewalk. "I had to have what I wanted & I got it. All I had to do was betray my mother." Eventually the golden boy found himself suffering in "the upper depths," a world ruled by sex, drugs, bulimia, blackouts, insomnia, trembling fits, and nightmares. He finally pulled himself together, earned a Ph.D., became a teacher. Part of the healing process was going back to those provinces to confront "the life I lived in cahoots with my childhood."

A word of advice before you begin to write. Tell it as it was, or at least the way you think it was. If your mother had more spiky idiosyncrasies than a porcupine, it would be best to show them. In her memoir *ME ME ME ME Not a Novel*, M.E. Kerr, a successful author of young adult novels, says whatever truce was reached between her and her mother—who thought she had missed the boat—was reached late in life. "What boat is that?" Kerr once asked. "You know very well what boat," Mrs. Kerr replied. "It's the same boat my grandchildren would be on. You missed that boat."

Beverly Cleary's memoir, *My Own Two Feet*, worked for the same reason her children's books did. She remembers the intense fears and the miserable humiliations of childhood.

The vivid pieces of reality become the classics, not the sentimentalized cubes of sugar. Leave the candy-coated stories for the romance novels. A writer's need for a "happy-ever-after" ending in fiction shows distrust of a reader's imagination, and reveals the writer's own lack of creativity. A memoir, especially one centering on your family, in which everything and everyone appears just dandy is apt to reek of the denial of an unexamined life.

Since it's harder to blame them for all our shortcomings and setbacks, uncles, aunts, cousins, and sometimes even siblings can lighten up the grimest family memoir. Russell Baker's uncle Harold, who was famous for lying, said he had been shot right between the eyes in World War I, but assured the young Russell marines were so tough they didn't need miracles to survive such an ordeal.

My heart hurt for Dylan Thomas's aunts: "Some few small aunts, not wanted in the kitchen, nor anywhere else for that matter, sat on the very edges of their chairs, poised and brittle, afraid to break, like faded cups and saucers." But as he remembers his Christmas in Wales, and especially his uncles, he could have been describing what happened at my house, or maybe yours: "For dinner we had turkey and blazing pudding, and after dinner the uncles sat in front of the fire, loosened all buttons, put their large moist hands over their watch chains, groaned a little and slept."

Michael Korda's uncles, especially his uncle Alex, didn't do mundane things like snore and snort. They made movies like *Cry the Beloved Country* that became classics and they married beautiful stars like Merle Oberon. When Korda recorded his memories of his father and his father's flamboyant brothers in *Charmed Lives*, Irwin Shaw said Korda had written with love, a clear eye, and an undeceived ear about, not one, but a whole family of Cinderellas who somehow, anyhow, kept the coach and horses from ever turning into a pumpkin at midnight.

My uncle Fehrn made me feel like Cinderella. He had sexy brown eyes and was a ladies' man. When people didn't do it, he got divorced four times. Between wife number three and number four, when I was eleven, on Saturday nights he used to take me out for dinner to restaurants that had linen tablecloths.

I do not have the powers of a mind reader or psychic, but I can imagine at this moment you are thinking: I can't, I couldn't, I shouldn't. . . . Dylan Thomas might have been able to admit in print that his auntie Hannah, who liked port, stood in the snowbound backyard "singing like a big-bosomed thrush," but if I were to tell some of the real stories about members of my family, I would be struck by lightning. Probably you wouldn't. Pull the blinds. Cover your work with your hand as you did in fifth grade math when you sat next to that kid who copied. Try some of the following exercises, and if nothing drastic happens, add some of your own.

## FAMILIES

- ☞ In our family . . . was comic relief.
- ☞ My grandmother/grandfather saved the day.
- ☞ What my father never understood was . . .
- ☞ I still can't forgive my brother/sister for . . .
- ☞ When my brother/sister left home, I . . .
- ☞ As soon as I had carved out my niche, they had another kid.
- ☞ I loved him and was ashamed of him.

☞  I had many cousins, but . . . was the best/worst.

☞  I married a man just like my father who belittled me and never gave me support.

☞  My brother/sister was not a bad seed as everyone said, but a symptom bearer of what was wrong in our family.

☞  My family was haunted by unmourned, unresolved sorrows and miseries of the past.

☞  Being the firstborn/baby/middle child had its advantages/disadvantages.

☞  Being a spoiled child might have been enjoyable, but later it caused him many problems.

☞  The quality of family life completely changed after . . .

☞  My family had been in the grips of an unconscious fantasy for generations.

☞  Political discussions in my family were . . .

☞  The funniest-looking relative I had was . . .

☞  The relative I wish I resembled is . . .

☞  Unfortunately . . . and . . . never got along.

☞  I knew my father/husband had wanted a boy.

☞  My parents were so puritanically frugal, I grew up thinking we were poor.

☞  My parents made me feel so secure, I grew up thinking we were rich.

☞  . . . was my mother's/father's favorite child.

☞  Religion was/was not important in my family.

☞  My father was determined I would . . . but I wasn't interested.

☞  I vowed when I had children I would never . . .

☞  After he died, the will caused hard feelings.

☞  I don't think my mother/father ever really wanted children.

☞  My parents approved/disapproved of my husband/wife.

☞  One day I finally told my son/daughter the statute of limitations on parental blame had run out.

☞  . . . is a family tradition my children still demand we observe.

☞  I remember a time when blood was not thicker than water.

☞  His most embarrassing habit was . . .

☞  The secret my family always tried to hide . . .

☞  Her manners and taste made me cringe.

# Chapter 9
## Families of Choice

*His ancient, trusty, drouthy crony:*
*Tam lo'ed him like a vera brither—*

—"Tam o'Shanter," Robert Burns

Families don't always work out. When I was growing up on an Illinois farm, we had a stubborn duck who insisted upon raising the baby chickens. An elitist ewe rejected her little black sheep, and one of our old sows ate all of her babies.

Blood relatives can let us down, die, desert us. We desert them for big cities with opportunities. But even if we grew up thinking the stork had left us on the wrong doorstep, most of us have a natural instinct to bond. Surrogate families can pop up in the wiggiest places with the most unlikely members. Look at your neighborhood, club, golf buddies. Church is a likely place, but so is your local pub. Thousands of people did not watch "Cheers" on television all those years just because the bartender was good-looking. The show struck a cord. If you didn't belong to a group like that, you could hang out with Sam and his quirky customers. Pretending is not as risky as sticking your neck out.

Last summer, the moment I handed the rental agent the security deposit, I panicked.

Ten unrelated people, uptown and downtown New Yorkers, living in one house? On a tiny island in Maine? I must be mad. Trying to picture the mix—prim, prime, primal, pushy, shy, and untamed—as a congenial group insinuated central casting, or I, had gone haywire.

Chip had a young heart, but he'd thrown a fiftieth birthday bash three or four years ago. Jim hadn't been shaving more than three or four years. The women, those who told their age, were in their thirties and forties. One shopped at Saks; her roommate preferred Second-Time-Around. One retired at ten; her roommate preferred wee-hour clubs. There were those who loved to cook and eat and those who looked askance as they jogged out the door. Sexually, they were gay, straight, and undeclared.

Our time together was not like a spotless white shirt. Some days left removable smudges, but no permanent stains. It worked. They have stuck together, celebrating when Maria got a new job, lamenting when Jessey and Tom had to move away, mourning when Keith's father died. They came back this summer. Next year there will be two groups. This unlikely entourage had one common bond, more than some blood relatives. They all were writers.

Who would have thought your investment club, women's luncheon group, mutual gym memberships, would have lasted this long? What brought you together and what has held you together could be an interesting story. It might have begun simply as an annual block party, but think of all you have been through since.

If you grew up as I did in a small town where everyone called you by your first name and the bank would cash your checks because they knew your dad, moving to the city is shocking. We reach out for people with common interests, hoping for more. Several years ago, homesick for the University of Chicago—some things, you never get over—I started a great-books discussion group for New York alumni. It's not quite a family, but it's more than a club. We bicker about book choices, become impatient when someone takes too long to say too little, but when

I've seen a good movie or play, want to share the joy of a special book, I call Kelly, Judy, Laura, Peter, Bruce, Robert, and appreciate my good fortune.

I've known grandmothers who still meet with the women they met daily in the park when their kids were in strollers. I no longer remember why we started The Hi-Gal Club when I was thirteen, but we vowed to stick together forever and we have, across state lines. The telephone company has been glad we did. A friend from the Philadelphia Main Line has continued for forty years to meet in a monthly discussion group with men from his Princeton class. There still being members of his class around doesn't surprise me since, as a reader of novels, I've always assumed all men from the Philadelphia Main Line went to Princeton. Taking summer shares in houses in the Hamptons is a New York phenomenon that has resulted in families of choice that continue to support each other, share holidays, long after the lifeguards fold their umbrellas on Long Island.

When you have the blues, need to confess, want to brag to those who will put up with it, but you would perish if anyone in the family knew, whom do you call? Blow the dust off the memories of how you met these people who have become your family because you chose them.

## FAMILIES OF CHOICE

☞ It began when we did a play together.

☞ It was in the days when all good mothers went to PTA meetings.

☞ We thought we were joining the country club just to have a place to play golf.

☞ After we had gone through the hurricane/fire/flood, we . . .

☞ At first we were a group of strangers who came together because we:

liked to play cards
loved the opera

preferred jazz

wanted to learn to dance

had a problem to solve

had children the same age

had all worked for . . . in the good/bad days

had season tickets to . . .

had the same disease

had joined/been drafted into the service

had spouses who . . .

had moved into the same building, neighborhood

had rented summer cottages at . . .

had endured domestic/sexual abuse

joined a professional organization

supported the same candidate

all collected . . .

all owned '57 T-birds, Airstreams, mountain bikes, snowmobiles

went on the same tour/cruise

were all going through a divorce

were scheduled into the same class

were all recovering alcoholics, drug abusers

were raising money for . . .

wanted to change . . .

wanted to lose weight

# Chapter 10
## Choices

*In the choice of a horse and a wife, a man must please himself, ignoring the opinion and advice of friends.*

—Riding Recollections,
  *George John Whyte-Melville*

We do not have choices about whose genes will create us, what size shoe we will wear, but we do make choices, sometimes unaware, that affect our accomplishments, our opportunities, and other people's lives. Someone wise said it's too bad education is wasted on the young. Someone wise should also have said hindsight helps about as much as rain after the crops have withered in the field.

Recently my friend Barbara was telling me about *Apollo 13*, a film in which a NASA engineer saved astronauts' lives by coming up with a way for them to fit a round filter into a square opening. "I wish I had a ground crew," she said. This is a woman who has begun to feel she has paid too high a price to be successful in a field where she doesn't fit and can no longer remember why she chose it in the first place.

Choices, what we did and the "might have beens," have shaped our lives. A very attractive, persuasive marine, who looked terrific in her snappy uniform, recruited on campus when I was eighteen. I came within a hair of signing on. What if the first woman you proposed to had said yes? What if you had given acting a go? Remember when you thought about buying stock in a company called Haloid that would later be renamed Xerox, but you chose not to take a risk on high tech?

Fortunately, most of us never consciously face as dramatic a decision as *Sophie's Choice*, but often in retrospect, we question how much of what happens is chance: Do we have free will, or is everything predetermined? When I was a stewardess, my roommate, Ruthie, was scheduled to work a trip from Chicago to Las Vegas, but another stewardess asked her to trade trips. Ruthie didn't want to swap. Vegas was a good layover town. The hotel always treated the crew to dinner and a show. But the other stew had a boyfriend out there, so reluctantly Ruthie agreed to switch. Ruthie was in dispatch checking in for the traded trip when we heard the bulletin. Two planes—one her original trip—had an unprecedented midair collision near Las Vegas. Both crews and all of the passengers were killed.

Looking not only at the choices you have made, but analyzing why you made them and how they turned out, could also add another piece to the philosophical puzzle you've been putting together most of your life, at least since those all-night discussions that began in the dorm your first year in college. Thomas Hardy felt it did not make much difference what choices his characters, Jude and Tess, made. They were fated to be defeated. But Shakespeare believed Othello did not have to assume Iago was telling the truth. If he had not reacted jealously, he would have chosen to fire that troublemaker Iago and Desdemona could have lived to play with her grandchildren.

Choices—cause and effect—are the essence not only of great literature, but the structure of our lives. Maybe it's time to examine the consequences of some of the roads you did and did not take—on paper, of course.

# CHOICES

☞   I had other offers, but I chose . . .

☞   I could have fired her, but I chose not to do so.

☞   I could have left him, but I didn't.

☞   I could have had an abortion.

☞   If I had told, I could have ruined him.

☞   I could have overlooked the affair, but I didn't.

☞   I could have been more gracious.

☞   I could never whip up any interest in the family business, but . . .

☞   My closet was full of options, but I chose to wear . . .

☞   There were many other places the money could have been used, but I chose to . . .

☞   I joined the army to avoid . . .

☞   My sister was the good girl, so I consciously chose to be the bad girl.

☞   I chose to go to college at . . . because . . .

☞   I majored in . . . because . . .

☞   I did it because I wanted to please.

☞   I did it because I was afraid.

☞   I did it to show . . . I could.

☞   I did it to pay her back.

☞   I did it because I was too young to know better.

☞   I did it to make money.

☞   I did it because I had the power.

☞   I did it because I could not see the long-range consequences.

☞   I accepted him so I wouldn't lose her.

☞   I went with him because no one else asked.

☞   I never returned the call.

☞   The cure seemed worse than the disease.

☞   I never told him/her.

☞   I returned the letter unopened.

# Chapter 11
# Regrets

*When I saw my wife again standing
by the tracks as the train came in
by the piled logs at the station, I
wished I had died before I ever
loved anyone but her.*

—A Moveable Feast,
*Ernest Hemingway*

Most of us have enough regrets to paper the Pentagon. We lament what we did or did not do, what we said or what we wished we had said. Remember the thank-you note you never wrote, the gift you never sent and now it's too late, or how you always meant to let him know how much he meant to you, how much you appreciated her help?

Think of the courses we didn't take in school because they were demanding, or maybe we declared with shaky conviction that they were boring. Friends and family who fear my ignorance might bring bodily harm to them, me, or property worth preserving have offered to pay tuition for me to take just one physics course, even at this late date. How many business opportunities have you missed because you never did schedule those tennis lessons you had planned, take that French class, or learn to use a computer or fax machine?

Those of us who aren't perfect have a stack of major and minor regrets, especially for having acted or reacted too quickly, especially when our blood was flowing hot. I've chased the postman down the block in my robe many mornings, hoping to retrieve a letter written the night before. Think of the mornings you've awakened with a thud thinking, Oh no, last night did I really tell Sadie I thought she should know Arthur was having an affair? Surely I didn't let Steve, of all people, know how much I hate my boss? Why would I have told him I knew how to do that report, when I haven't a clue even where to start? How will I ever explain having overdrawn our joint account again? Why did I accept the invitation when I knew how uncomfortable I would be with those people? I accepted the chairman's role for all the wrong reasons.

In retrospect, many regrets give us fodder for funny memoirs—the awkward vacuum cleaner you bought because the salesman was good-looking, the date you turned down because your shoes were killing you, the disastrous assistant you hired because she liked your tie, the ghastly green noodle casserole you've endured for ten years because of an encouraging remark to your bride, a ride-to-work agreement you made because you didn't want to hurt your talky neighbor's feelings. Look at some of the disasters hanging in your closet, and the furniture you've bumped into for ten years because it always was too big for the space, but you couldn't admit you had used bad judgment, especially to your mother-in-law. And how about the ghastly bedroom wallpaper that was so expensive you've had to go to bed dizzy for ten years.

Other regrets cut deeper: the time we did not spend with someone who died before we expected it; evidence like a child's abusing dope or alcohol we couldn't bear to face; an affair we never should have started and let go too far; a financial decision we knew was a gamble. A lie that seemed like a good idea at the time has lashed back to bite many sorry souls. A truth there was no need to tell may have backfired too.

Some old saws, such as "if we don't learn from our mistakes, we will repeat them," can't be improved. Look at the people you know whose second marriage is cruising toward the same iceberg that sunk the first one, or listen to the mouthy guy who lost his last job for not knowing when to be quiet, or the woman wearing her tattered heart on her sleeve in yet another relationship where she is still trying too hard.

After four marriages, even proud Mr. Hemingway might have had some regrets. Whether he learned from his mistakes or simply became nostalgic and sentimental as he grew older is debatable, however. *A Moveable Feast* reads like a love letter to Hadley, his first wife and mother of his son, John (Bumby). But Papa and humility were never on friendly terms. He blames the predatory rich—his second wife, Pauline Pfeiffer, Gerald and Sara Murphy—not himself, for destroying his marriage to Hadley.

You don't have to have fought bulls in Spain, shot tigers in Africa, or had four marriages to write a memoir. Fighting the snakes in your office, keeping the family together without the aid of a gun or a divorce lawyer, could have taken just as much courage—maybe more. With so much material to draw upon, why add another regret to the list? If you have old scores to settle and are thinking about retaliation or vengeance, it could feel good to put it on paper, but talking to a shrink might be wiser than looking for a publisher.

An old proverb says, "If it's revenge you want, dig two graves."

Few people had anything good to say about Georgia Power when she wrote her kiss-and-tell memoir about Martin Luther King Jr., *I Shared the Dream: The Pride, Passion & Politics of the First Black Woman Senator from Kentucky*. Pulitzer Prize winner Isabel Wilkerson said in her *New York Times* review:

> There are few human gods in a given century. But if there have been any in ours, Martin Luther King Jr. is surely among them. For years, though, there were whispers that King had his dalliances, which were recorded by a government that trailed his every move. But who would set such things to paper, raise her hand and tell the world that she carried on with a saint, decades after the fact and with his widow alive and still grieving besides?

Granted the senator had suffered the indignities of being the other woman. She writes of one such incident that happened after King was shot. Power had begun to climb into the ambulance with him until Andrew Young, a King lieutenant, said: "No, Senator. I don't think you want to do that." But reading her words, Wilkerson and others felt she knew precisely what she was doing and had few regrets. One wonders if she had any regrets after the reviews.

Around the same time critics were saying *tsk tsk* to Powers, Mary Karr's gritty story *The Liar's Club*, a memoir of her East Texas childhood, received excellent reviews. When Karr began her tale, Tobias Wolff, author of *This Boy's Life*, the story of his own harsh upbringing, told her in a letter, "Don't approach history as something to be shaken for its cautionary fruits. Don't be afraid of appearing angry, small-minded, obtuse, mean, immoral, amoral, calculating or anything else," Wolff wrote. "Take no care of your dignity." Karr didn't.

The story of her childhood in a town in the "Texas Ringworm Belt" that *Business Week* labeled one of the ten ugliest on the planet took its title from an actual club Karr's father belonged to. The blatantly honest tone came from Karr, raised by a mother insensible from drugs and alcohol, who married six times. Karr was physically abused, molested, raped before she learned her multiplication tables. Forsaking prudence, Karr also wrote about the wild romp she went on after leaving home.

Unlike Power's, Karr's story does not smack of revenge, nor does it seem self-serving. In her *New York Times* review, Dinitia Smith said, "In a way *The Liar's Club* is a helpless child's answer to a mother before whom she is powerless. A quest for the truth about her family was a search for salvation. And in a way it redeemed her mother's life as well."

Even though reading the many newspapers geared to sensational stories could lead one to believe Karr's life fits a norm, your less lurid stories will also find an audience. There are still Jane Austen readers.

When my friend Katie, who had had the least bumpy marriage of us all, discovered her husband—the most dependable guy in the world—was having an affair, I thought she was going to crack up. Then a wise counselor told her,

"You want me to make it not have happened. I can't do that, but I can help you to build a new life, starting today." Katie finally let go of her regrets, got a job, made some new friends, raised a healthy son. If you don't have a wise adviser on call, laying your regrets out on paper could be cathartic. There could still be time to make it better.

What I liked about the sixties was the sense of hope of making it better. In 1970 a small publisher in Moab, Utah, bought *Notes to Myself: My Struggle to Become a Person,* by little-known author Hugh Prather. With no promotion, just word of mouth, it sold over one million copies. It opens with:

> *If I had only . . .*
> *forgotten future greatness*
> *and looked at the green things and the buildings*
> *and reached out to those around me*
> *and smelled the air*
> *and ignored the forms and the self-styled obligations*
> *and heard the rain on the roof*
> *and put my arms around my wife*
> *. . . and it's not too late.*

Writing about our accomplishments is easier than facing our regrets. The hidden and the avoided grow more powerful. The unknown scares us. But ferreting out shards of our past to be reexamined can rub the edges into smooth beach glass. And it might not be too late. Be brave. You will probably have another thing to lament if you don't.

Writing one of the following could give you that epiphany you need to improve your judgment or shoo away old ghosts who have hung around too long.

## REGRETS

☞   If I had only taken the time to . . .

☞   If I had it to do over, I'd . . .

☞   Now I wish I had punched him in the nose.

☞   I could have made more friends if I had . . .

☞ I should have reported her.

☞ I had no idea how much I'd miss him until . . .

☞ My mother/father tried to tell me I'd be sorry if I quit.

☞ I didn't realize how lonely I would be until . . .

☞ I let pride ruin my chance to . . .

☞ I lost a friend when I told her something she did not want to know.

☞ I overreacted.

☞ I wish I had faced my dependency earlier.

☞ I should have saved . . .

☞ Back then I couldn't see beyond the end of my nose.

☞ Believing/trusting him was the worst mistake I ever made.

☞ She would have been better served knowing from the beginning she was adopted.

☞ I only thought everyone would forget/forgive.

☞ I let it get out of hand.

☞ When he wanted to . . . I should have agreed.

☞ Then he died and it was too late.

☞ At first it was a lark, now it's an addiction.

☞ I did not realize how much I would miss my kids.

☞ At that time an abortion was socially unacceptable.

☞ I never saw him pitch one game.

☞ I should have invited them to our house.

☞ She would have forgiven me if I had . . .

☞ At her wedding, I kept thinking it could've been me.

☞ I should not have had that last drink.

☞ I wish I had not been so concerned about saving money.

☞ I didn't like football/racing/bridge because I didn't understand it, but I could have learned.

☞ I should have told her what a good job she was doing/ how proud I was.

# Chapter 12
# Missed Opportunities

*I could've been a contender.*

—On the Waterfront

If you had been three inches taller, you might have been an astronaut as you had planned since Neil Armstrong walked on the moon. Of course, if you had been three inches shorter, you could have ridden in the Kentucky Derby, maybe won the Triple Crown. If your father hadn't lost his money in that real estate swindle, you could have gone to Harvard and who knows what might have happened. Fantasies feed our souls.

In this land of promised opportunity for all, Americans grow up on inspiring stories about Lana Turner being discovered at a soda fountain, poor children being endowed by rich philanthropists, the ambitious young being mentored into greatness by the powerful. Those of us who write glom on to tales like Saul Bellow asking his editor to read William Kennedy's Pulitzer Prize-winning *Ironweed* after it had been rejected a couple of dozen times, or Walker Percy's recognizing the excellence in John Kennedy Toole's

*A Confederacy of Dunces* years after Toole's publisher had welshed on their deal and he had taken his own life.

Hope motivates us to turn on the computer, board the train, pick up the shovel, lower the gavel. If other people's miracles help you to keep the faith, good for you. Whatever works.

However, in this section I have made a distinction among daydreams, real choices you made, and actual opportunities missed when the circumstances were beyond your control. Irony usually figures in all three situations, but missed opportunities might be more fun to write since you can put the blame on an indifferent universe rather than yourself.

## MISSED OPPORTUNITIES

- ☞ I got drafted.

- ☞ She took a seat right next to me, but then it was my subway stop.

- ☞ Five more points was all it would have taken.

- ☞ Early on, he had asked me to join his team, but I had no way of knowing . . .

- ☞ It got lost in the mail.

- ☞ It was stolen.

- ☞ He was sterile.

- ☞ The recruiter had an obvious racial/sexual bias.

- ☞ I almost bought it at . . . but then I had to pay my son's tuition.

- ☞ My plane was late, so it went to . . .

- ☞ The lost bag containing my novel/dissertation/business plan was never found.

- ☞ By the time I finished it, someone else's idea had been accepted.

- ☞ I had agreed to relocate, but then my father died.

☞ It was just a silly accident, but it ruined my audition.

☞ She didn't give me the message.

☞ He didn't leave a message.

☞ At that time, the doctor said a hysterectomy was the only option.

☞ I broke my arm a week before tryouts.

☞ The fire destroyed all the records.

☞ The security check hit a ridiculous snag.

☞ No one else showed up.

☞ The other party upped their bid beyond my means.

☞ The judge threw out the case.

☞ My competitor lied.

☞ The power outage only lasted seconds, but I was never able to retrieve the file.

☞ The patch indicated I was ovulating, but he was out-of-town.

☞ He was dead by the time I learned.

# Chapter 13
# Shame, Embarrassment, Confusion

*The mass of men live lives of quiet desperation.*

—Walden, *Henry David Thoreau*

Advertising agencies cut and splice to remove bloopers in commercials. Movie and stage actors rehearse until they get it right. Professors give review courses for law and medical qualifying exams. Editors clean up manuscripts. But we pull a boner and it's a wrap.

Having something embarrassing happen is the loneliest feeling. You are sure no one has ever done anything as stupid as forgetting to pick up your kids after soccer, having the elastic in your underwear snap when you're giving a speech, calling your husband by an old boyfriend's name, panicking while making an important presentation, leaving the car windows down in a rainstorm, not remembering your anniversary, forgetting to write the check, drinking too much at a wedding, losing your tickets, not writing down the date, spilling your wine on the white linen tablecloth. Relax. If confessing embarrassing moments were the price of admission, there would always be a full house.

You might not have forgotten one tiny detail about those mortifying moments, but you would be surprised how little anyone else remembers. Other people's boners are much easier to bear. Besides, think of the material those incidents have given you for your memoir.

In an earlier section, we looked at how family members had caused you shame and embarrassment, which is hard to handle, but it's even more painful when you let yourself or others down. Taking what wasn't yours, bankruptcy, the fifth, drugs, getting fired, being a schmuck, getting a divorce, ducking responsibility, were not on your original To Do List, but things happen. They are universal problems. The Greeks began writing plays about the same conflicts and flaws in man's character 450 years before Christ. Looking at how, why, and what it means to you is a healthy way to recover.

The oracle has left Delphi. There are so many things, not only about ourselves but our world, we don't understand. Only in sitcoms can problems be solved, confusion made clear, and people find a way to live happily ever after in an hour of prime time. These pop culture escape vehicles do not answer our questions. Why do bad people get ahead, or away with murder? Why do good people become corrupted by power?

Writing about the things that have made you feel chagrin or mortified might be like cleaning out the junk drawer. Putting puzzling ideas, questions, and happenings into words might help to clear the muck.

## SHAME, EMBARRASSMENT, CONFUSION

☞   I tripped.

☞   I forgot.

☞   I dropped it.

☞   I lost it.

☞   My mind went blank.

☞ It was gooey in the middle.

☞ The zipper broke.

☞ No one chose me.

☞ I came in last.

☞ I thought I would never be able to hold my head up again.

☞ Now I can't even remember why I was tempted.

☞ When my wife found out, she . . .

☞ The suicide confused me as much as it hurt.

☞ Having to seek help hurt my pride.

☞ I did not put it on my resume.

☞ I worked hard, but could not get ahead.

☞ No one could believe it when he was promoted/got the appointment.

☞ He had more than his share.

☞ I did exactly what I was told.

☞ Money was the problem.

☞ The rejection letter did not make sense.

☞ When my friends bragged about their children, I tried subtly to change the subject.

☞ I am still convinced my entry was the best.

☞ No one would ever tell me what I did wrong.

☞ I didn't realize it was a preengagement ring.

☞ I didn't know my own strength.

☞ It wouldn't wash off.

☞ I forgot the test was scheduled for Friday.

# Chapter 14
## Accomplishments

*In the long run men hit only what they aim at.*

—Walden, *Henry David Thoreau*

When Sunday school teachers said, "Blessed are the meek, for they shall inherit the earth," young Lee Iacocca, Donald Trump, Newt Gingrich, Norman Schwarzkopf, obviously didn't believe them, but many—particularly nice girls—did, especially when the maxim was reinforced at home with "Don't blow your own horn." I must have written, with ease, a trillion glowing letters of recommendation for my students, but still tend to sell myself as too many women of my generation do: "I don't suppose you would want . . ."

Those of us who buy our bagels by writing find it especially offensive when the less than modest publish a book written by a ghost or "with so and so" but immediately forget they hired someone to blow their horn and push the pen.

Stand a little taller. You are going to write your own story. Don't skip the things that make you proud as well as the missteps.

Equating bragging with taking credit is like comparing a balloon to a dirigible. When you gave yourself permission to write, including achievements came with the package. Don't fret if you have not been elected to an office since you were treasurer of the eighth grade chess club or haven't been awarded the Medal of Honor, the Nobel, Pulitzer, or the Miss America crown. If you have raised respectable children, survived a tyrant at home or in the office, taken care of aging parents, become successful without lying, cheating, or stealing, you deserve acknowledgment.

Good writers pay unflappable attention to the stuff of everyday life—the daily decencies and indecencies of husbands and wives, the ongoing frustrations of too little money and too many temptations. Gwendolyn Brooks's "bean eaters" are an old couple who have lived their day, but they keep on doing routine things like getting dressed and putting things away.

If I were recruiting for a position wherein character was the main concern, I would ask the applicant how long she had been able to keep the same housekeeper.

I usually like people who have kept in touch with their best friend in third grade.

One of my best friends is president of a college, another knits beautiful sweaters and can cook like Julia Child. Both are accomplished women.

If you grew up in a family that abused each other, harmful substances, or the system, but you managed not to follow the pattern, you deserve recognition. If you can describe your family without using the weary word *dysfunctional,* that is also an accomplishment.

If you are one of those bosses whose employees like you, I not only want to read your memoir, I want to have lunch.

An artist friend spends many afternoons walking the Maine shore. She picks up rocks, driftwood, twigs, beach glass, to make not-what-you-expect arrangements in her studio and home. The weathered wheelbarrow in the living room sometimes is filled with fat rocks with white stripes around their middle like pigs. Sometimes it holds ancient books with cracked leather bindings and handmade paper, or a tub of ditch flowers. Only one side of a very old rocker rests on a high shelf. She has an eye.

Maybe you have an artistic eye that can make a basic

black dress proud with a string of amber beads and an unmatched pair of earrings, or turn a rectanguler room, bland as a boxcar, into a cozy living space. If you have turned ten tall, stringy, awkward adolescents into a basketball team, now that's an accomplishment.

When my nephew Dannon was an adolescent, he moved with his family into an affluent neighborhood in an Iowa town where many families had basements finished elegantly. For four years his mother, my sister, fretted as twelve to twenty of Dannon's friends trooped through her kitchen daily on their way down to hers, where in the winter they had to wrap themselves in blankets because there was no heat, the walls were cement, some moving cartons were still stashed under the pool table. When the kids left for college, another mother, one with a pine-paneled, heated rec room that had been empty for four years, asked, "We—the other mothers and I—have always wondered what you did. Why did the boys always come to your house after practice, on weekends?"

Some people—maybe you—have a talent for putting together a  dinner party guest list where the main course is electrifying conversation, or maybe you have a better track record for matchmaking than Cupid. Take credit, or consider one of the following:

## ACCOMPLISHMENTS

- ☞ No one, including me, thought I had a chance.
- ☞ The most difficult test I ever passed . . .
- ☞ The competition frightened me.
- ☞ It was the most demanding position I've filled.
- ☞ She said she could not have done it without me.
- ☞ My mother kept a scrapbook.
- ☞ The prize changed my life.
- ☞ We have been friends forever.
- ☞ We started out in the red.
- ☞ My children come home.

☞ They put it on display.

☞ They depend on me.

☞ They were prouder than I was.

☞ Training that mutt was not easy.

☞ It took all the willpower I could muster.

☞ I kicked the habit.

☞ I stuck by him.

☞ I won a scholarship.

☞ I worked my way through.

☞ I took a stand.

☞ I took his advice.

☞ I refused to rat.

☞ I didn't look the part.

☞ I did not deny my past.

☞ I did not let it get me down.

☞ I gave credit to those who did the work.

☞ I never lie about my age or weight.

☞ I recognized her talent early.

☞ I worked hard on overcoming my bias.

☞ I overcame an unattractive family pattern.

☞ I convinced her to change her mind.

☞ I always remember where I came from.

☞ I put up with her for twenty years.

☞ I was the youngest person to have . . .

☞ I was the first African-American, American Indian, Asian, female, Catholic, Jew, white male, person over sixty, to . . .

☞ I got a bellyful of turning the other cheek.

☞ I had decided what I wanted to be/do when I was a child.

☞ I contributed even though it meant giving up things I enjoyed.

☞ I made every dime I have.

☞ I have friends who have never made a dime.

☞ I accomplished my dream.

---

# Chapter 15
# Point of View, Tone, and Voice

*I touch the future. I teach.*

*—Christa McAuliffe*

When Muhammad Ali said, "I am the greatest," he got away
with it because he said it with a twinkle in his eye. Learning to write about yourself and your life so the twinkle in
your eye shows is our mission.

Writing anything—a memo, letter, travel article, novel,
memoir—is selling. You're trying to sway someone to believe what you say is true or to buy your idea, opinion,
view of the Himalayas or the human condition. Voice and
tone, the basic components of viewpoint, can make or
break the sale.

You choose to listen to Barbra Streisand or Carolyn
Horn. Think of the choices you have made in the voting
booth. Can you still remember the appeal or repulsion you
heard in the voices of Richard Nixon, John Kennedy, Ronald Reagan, Jimmy Carter? Writers, like you, develop
voices that are as recognizable as singers and politicians.
The voices reveal attitude.

Tone designates the attitude the speaker (narrator) has toward his subject, his audience, and—especially in a memoir—himself. The emotional and intellectual effect of our writing on the reader is also to a large extent determined by tone. It isn't necessary to berate yourself as British editor Frank Kermode did in his memoir *Not Entitled,* but nothing puts a reader off more than a writer who obviously thinks he is a hotshot. The tone, set by the speaker or writer's voice, can reflect the entire range of human emotions and attitudes: formal, intimate, solemn, serious, angry, bitter, comic, cheerful, ironic, condescending, obsequious. When you get it wrong, it can be arrogant, a tone that can intimidate, but persuades only the toadies.

The best voice sounds natural and honest, as it does in literature. Actors often make the mistake of trying to answer the tabloid scandals by writing memoirs too self-protective to be real, but the worst are politicians' books, the ones that sound as if they have been rehearsed and recited.

Reviewing several "small" (his word) TV stars' memoirs for *The New Yorker,* James Wolcott contended "these phonies" never told the truth. He said Mary Tyler Moore had threatened to empty the cupboard in her desire to be real. "Why bother? If we wanted honest-to-God literature, we'd go to—literature. They keep that in a different section of the superstore." Wolcott's voice sounds as if he's been drinking vinegar, but pay attention to his disdain. When you choose your subject, pick one you will feel comfortable telling the way you remember it—all of it. Even with safety filters, the truth usually shows through.

For a quick lesson in understanding the importance of voice and tone, read newspaper columnists. They write immediate mini memoirs twice a week expressing their personal opinions of people, places, and events.

You don't have to be introduced to know a writer. Some have the uncanny ability to bring the reader inside their own skin, like former *New York Times* columnist, now novelist, Anna Quindlen, whose tone is intimate, no matter the topic. You fall into a seamless identification with her, the narrator. She told her readers when her husband said, "Could you get up and get me a beer without writing about it?" We weren't surprised because she had already said men fall into two categories: husbands and boyfriends, and she had married a boyfriend. Quindlen's tone reflects self-confidence as well as humor and honesty.

Quindlen's replacement at *The Times*, Maureen Dowd, is wise not to write much about her family. She would not have any place to go for Christmas. Dowd appears never to have met anyone she wouldn't like to put down, even those of her political persuasion, but especially President Clinton and his first lady. In 1995 on an international trip, when the president was receiving press adulation on his visit to Ireland, she quoted London's *Daily Telegram:* "Cherub-faced hick makes peace with the men in tights" (officials at Westminster). She uses a sharp knife to carve her sarcastic tone. Sarcasm is personal, jeering, intended to hurt like a sneering taunt.

I miss Anna, whose words seemed to come from her heart. I imagine Dowd takes pride in shooting from the hip, but she reminds me of the show-offs I used to meet on the playground.

Reporter and young adult novelist Robert Lipsyte has a quite healthy ego, but notice how, by writing a self-parody, he lets the reader know he is intelligent without sounding like a show-off or braggart. In a junior high memoir piece in the *New York Times* he said:

> At Halsey, I belonged to a group targeted by bullies. The members of the Special Progress class had been selected primarily by their above average I.Q. scores (120 was supposedly the cut-off), a fact we flaunted like a varsity letter. Not only were we smarter, but we were too cool for this school; we would leave for high school after completing the three-year curriculum in two. We were easy to resent.

Long after Lipsyte has lost weight and gained a reputation as a writer, he can also lampoon himself for being a fat kid and not a good fighter. As the spoof continues, the fat kid finally takes on Willy, the school bully, and wins (by falling on him) while we the readers are cheering for the smart, fat kid, just as Lipsyte had planned.

How we persuade ourselves we are worthy human beings doesn't often make it into print. James Joyce, William Faulkner, Virginia Woolf, knew how to turn their fictional characters' internal struggles (stream of consciousness) into almost rational thought, but many of us would prefer no one overhear the clashes between our self-admiration and self-doubt in which the former fights so valiantly to win so little ground. Then there is Gore Vidal, who would have no patience for such dithering.

I agree with Michael Wood's review of Vidal's memoir, *Palimpsest.* When he says Vidal's doubts are few and well disciplined, and his admiration for himself is frank and immense, but we part company when Wood suggests what would have come off as arrogance when Vidal was young, now that he's in his seventies, reads as self-admiration, but not self-absorption. The reviewer thought Vidal had written in a "disinterested" tone. I call it haughty.

In an interview around the time of publication, assuming the tone of his memoir, Vidal said when he was a child he wished his mother would die, but then most people who knew her well felt that way because she was actively malevolent. When asked if he didn't think it was time he finally met his cousin Albert Gore, Vidal replied that he had met far too many vice presidents as it was.

In a later section we will look at how putting others down doesn't always raise oneself above them, even when it is done with wit.

The cleverest advertising agency writers know how to set a tone, to find a voice that sells. Unless you make your living operating a jackhammer, your psyche is endlessly inundated with commercials, no matter how much you might abhor them. You might as well try to learn something useful from all that noise you endure. In a capitalistic country, it is disappointing, but not surprising, that ad agencies hire some of the best writers. A society that is not as literate as we wish only has a market for a limited number of Anne Tylers, Annie Dillards, and Anna Quindlens, and although writers are supposed to be willing to starve in a garret, most of us like steam heat and steamed lobsters as much as anyone.

"With a name like Smuckers, we have to be good" does not set my teeth on edge. I've heard it a hundred times and still appreciate the company's humor. As they satirize themselves, I feel as if we have shared a wink. By their not taking themselves so seriously, I smile and buy their strawberry jam. Compare the subtly ironic Smuckers tone to the loud bluster in "Nobody beats the Wiz." When I can't lower the radio volume quickly enough or find the television mute button, I think, Who says? and vow to find another place to buy my next piece of electronic equipment.

Words can swagger and strut as well as persuade and convince. They can also reflect the way you see yourself and the world you inhabit.

When the verdict for the infamous O.J. Simpson murder case came in, I was teaching a course at The New School, which is neither new nor a school, but a seventy-year-old university that attracts such an eclectic range of students, most classes could pass a political correctness test for diversity. When I asked my students to write their opinion on the verdict, I now wish I had taped their responses. I would never again have had to prepare a lecture on point of view. Shaking his head, David said, "Did we watch the same trial?" No. Their age, race, values, and experience shaped what they saw, heard, and believed to be true. We call that *viewpoint.*

Your impetus to record your memories will, of course, have the strongest effect on the tone and the voice. Reviewer Diane Johnson has said the impulse to write a memoir usually fits into one or more of three categories: revenge, witness, or self-justification. This brought to her mind *Mommy Dearest,* by Joan Crawford's daughter. I thought of *Passion and Prejudice,* by heiress Sallie Bingham, the daughter who set in motion the events that led to the $434 million divestment of the family's two Louisville, Kentucky, newspapers. Bingham wrote her story before the dust had settled. She might have been wise to observe the seven-year rule.

*This Boy's Life,* by Tobias Wolff, was published around the time the Bingham family's spat over their newspaper empire was making news and Bingham had given her side of the feud in print. I had liked one of Bingham's novels, she had given impressive sums of money to women's causes, and we had a mutual friend—reasons enough to go to hear her read at the West Side Y. Wolff, whose work I did not know at the time, was sharing the program. I can still recall the embarrassment I felt for this woman as she whined about her privileged life, paraded her feelings of sibling rivalry, and blamed her parents for her unfulfilling life. I am convinced she would have appeared spoiled and immature if she had been the only speaker, but the contrast to Wolff, who told the story of his father—an impostor and a bum—with humor, forgiveness, and even affection, highlighted the unpleasant tone from the lady who did protest too much. Bragging or complaining does not persuade.

I found Bingham's title, *Passion and Prejudice,* an obvious play on Jane Austen's *Pride and Prejudice,* as unwise a choice as her somber tone. Why encourage the reader to compare Austen's witty, ironic portrayal of the Bennet sisters' trials when dealing with the haughty and the empowered to the Bingham sisters' bathos?

Fiction writers hoping to make readers sympathetic to their characters, their perspective, and their story have many options when choosing their point of view and voice. For example, Fitzgerald, who had had his problems being snubbed by the rich, created a story about a man named Jay Gatsby whose life was destroyed by the insensitive East Coast old-money set. Fitzgerald was on Gatsby's side, even though this smooth bootlegger, too, had his flaws. No one would have been convinced if Gatsby had gone around saying, "I'm the greatest." He couldn't have managed a twinkle in his eye. Daisy, one of the upper crust, had broken his heart. Wisely, Fitzgerald chose to tell his tale from the point of view of dependable midwesterner Nick Carraway, a reliable, thoughtful narrator with a serious voice. Nick was so trustworthy he could not only get away with calling him the great Gatsby, but could even persuade the reader to agree with his perception.

Unfortunately, if you want to convince your readers you are the greatest, you are on your own. Memoir writers have only one vantage point—their own. Listening, as objectively as is possible, to your writer's voice can shock you into self-awareness in the same way as watching an audience's response to your speech or presentation. The advantage is, you can have your epiphany in the privacy of your study.

Frederick Busch found a clever way around the problem in "For the Love of a Princess of Mars," a short memoir for *The Threepenny Review.* He opens with: "It's 1949 or '50, and the kid's on his way to the East 12th Street branch of the Brooklyn Library." By creating this character, "the kid," he, the seasoned adult, can portray himself more affectionately and more humorously than if he said, "When I was a boy, being more sensitive than the others, I spent a lot of time at the library." In case there's any doubt about the kid's identity, midway through the essay he writes, "So every Friday night, he, becoming me, carried home a stack of six or seven books."

Writers become ventriloquists. Practice throwing your voice into one of the following situations:

## POINT OF VIEW, TONE, VOICE

☞ Describe your reaction to a circus clown, assuming the voice of:

> you as a child
> you in the present, attending under duress
> you in the present, in a jolly mood, with a companion you love

☞ Describe your backache:
> as if you were a curmudgeon
> as if you were trying to be a good sport
> as if you were a hypochondriac

☞ Describe your boss:

> to show your respect
> to show your disdain

☞ Describe your reaction to a Sunday sermon:

> when you have a hangover
> when you are worried about a serious problem

☞ Describe a hard-rock band:

> from your point of view
> from a young fan's perspective

☞ Describe yourself as a candidate for promotion:

> to show the confidence of a winner
> to show your insecurity

☞   You visit someone who is the proud owner of a new cat:

   write your reaction as if you are allergic to cats
   write your reaction as if you are a cat lover

☞   You drank all of the milk/didn't fill the gas tank:

   write your defense in dialogue
   write your admission in dialogue

☞   Write a description of a president:

   one from your party
   one from their party

# Chapter 16
## Irony

*I learned courage from Buddha,*
*Jesus, Lincoln, Einstein, and*
*Cary Grant.*

—*Peggy Lee*

Accounts of personal quests are often characterized by an air of high sincerity and insufficient irony. Rick Moody's short story "The Apocalypse Commentary of Bob Paisner" starts as every teacher's nightmare, when the protagonist turns in the kind of impossible self-reverential term paper that traces "the similarities between myself and Saint John the Divine."

When William Saroyan said he always knew everybody had to die but thought an exception would be made in his case, he didn't mean it. He was being ironic.

Verbal irony implies attitudes or evaluations opposed to those literally expressed. For example, if you say, "My dorm room was adequate. Six flights of stairs kept me in shape and the bedbugs kept me company," by *adequate,* you, of course, mean inadequate. Irony carries an implicit compliment to the intelligence of the reader who is associated with the knowing minority not taken in by the literal meaning.

When writing about yourself, irony is your best insurance against coming off as an egotistical bore.

Dramatic irony—a situation in which others are blind to facts known or recognized by the spectator or reader—is a very effective technique because it makes those in the know feel intelligent. Dramatic irony makes comedy popular. The observer or reader would know better than to believe the con, be taken in by mistaken identity, tell if he saw a unicorn in the garden, or cut down the cherry orchard.

When AT&T's monopoly on the telephone industry ended, competitors' wordsmiths went to work. For their spokesperson, one company hired an actress whose ironic voice was as familiar as a member of the family. The actress employed dramatic irony when she asked a series of befuddled people how much they were spending on long-distance calls. Turning back to you, her informed target, she implied with a knowing look that, of course, you understood as she did how perfectly silly it was for these baffled people to spend more with another company when they (and you) could save money with hers. In the visual commercial, however, the movie and television star also relied on her acting techniques—a shrug of the shoulders, a raised eyebrow—methods not available to the writer any more than the twinkle in an eye.

Russell Baker knows how to write with a twinkle in his eye. Known for his ironic voice, with a self-deprecating tone, Baker had been a highly respected and beloved columnist for *The New York Times* long before he wrote his memoir, *Growing Up*. Therefore, when he tells about his mother's concern that he would never make something of himself, the dramatic irony makes us feel way ahead of the sincere, but shortsighted, Lucy Elizabeth Baker, especially when, with a straight face and a serious tone, Baker writes: "The flaw in my character which she had already spotted was lack of 'gumption.' " After several flops at other jobs, he says: "So far as I could make out . . . writers didn't have to have any gumption at all. I did not dare tell anybody for fear of being laughed at in the schoolyard, but secretly I decided that what I'd like to be when I grew up was a writer."

In a condescending tone, Baker could have written something like: "Poor Mother thought I didn't have any gumption. I guess I showed her and the universe when I became a columnist for *The New York Times*, which just happens to be one of the best newspapers in the world." The superior attitude would not only have been patronizing to his mother, but also to his reader, who he would be assuming were stupid blokes who would have to be told what a glorious reputation he and his paper enjoyed.

Underplaying your accomplishments as Baker did works as long as your architecture doesn't show. Writers build their stories on techniques that must be as invisible as the beams in the supporting wall of your house. In a review of *Writing Was Everything*, noted critic Alfred Kazin was accused of being coy when he said, "I had to my surprise become a full-fledged professor at distinguished universities here and abroad." "To my surprise" comes off as sincere as a beauty pageant winner saying she had never thought she was attractive.

Understatement is a form of irony in which something is intentionally represented as less than it really is. The effect is often comic as in Twain's famous line: "The reports of my death are greatly exaggerated."

The cool writer of irony has her tongue in her cheek. The heated writer of sarcasm has meanness on his mind. George Will, another columnist, can occasionally stray across to the hot side of the street as in the piece "Shirley MacLaine: Hyperventilating in China." He wrote: "Back home, her consciousness raised, Ms. MacLaine made the long march to Las Vegas to put her art in the service of the masses."

The master of the caustic tone, however, is Gore Vidal, who cuts with the serious intent of revenge in *Palimpsest*. To pay back Charlton Heston for not having given Vidal credit for his work on the script of *Ben Hur*, he says directing Heston must be like trying "to animate an entire lumberyard."

Brazenly stretching the truth, like Vidal's comparison, can be used to heighten effect as well as to cut someone down. These bold, conscious exaggerations are not intended to be taken literally. Shakespeare must have especially liked his hyperbolic lines from *Richard II*, "Not all the waters in the rude rough sea/Can wash the balm from anointed King," since later he used the same idea in Macbeth: "Will all great Neptune's ocean wash this/blood/ Clean from my hand? No this my hand will/rather/ The multitudinous seas incarnadine/Making the green one red."

Mark Twain relied on extravagant hyperbolic statements for humor, such as the following entry in his notebook: "France has neither winter nor summer nor morals—apart from these drawbacks it is a fine country."

When Christopher Reeve, an actor known for his portrayal of Superman, was paralyzed from the neck down in an accident, he opened his remarks at an awards ceremony with hyperbole. Reeve, strapped in a wheelchair and breathing through a respirator, recalled his Princeton Day School dance teacher, alleged to have said that the only reason for not attending dance class was having a quadruple amputation, and even then they would bring you in a basket. Reeve then said, "I thought I had better show up tonight."

We pass for who we are, especially when we put it in writing. The tone you take in your memoir will tell more about you than the best photographer can capture. One of the things that still amazes me about writing is how much I learn about myself when I read what I write.

With a little luck, the most interesting character in your story will be you, the person who wrote the memoir. Learning to see when you have moved too close to the thin line separating ego from boring egotism, you will show how you have changed and grown, learned from this life. Before you begin to write, you might want to practice developing a viewpoint to avoid the narcissistic style by doing some of the exercises below.

The flower narcissus was named after the young man who pined away for love of his own reflection, and the word has come to mean vanity, self-love, and—worst of all for a writer—even to numb, to put to sleep.

# IRONY

☞ Describe the following in different tones reflecting irony, sarcasm, understatement, or hyperbole:

> your response when a friend or family member announced her engagement to a cad
>
> the love you feel for your child/grandchild/best friend/lover/spouse
>
> what you see when you brush your teeth or shave
>
> your feelings about telemarketing calls that come when you're having dinner/making love
>
> what you would say to an antagonistic in-law/boss/cousin if you had the nerve
>
> what you would say, given the opportunity, to the most annoying politician you've endured
>
> the proudest moment in your life
>
> what you do to make a living
>
> someone you admire

☞ Use irony to express how you feel about the following:

> Monday night football
>
> trumpet lessons you took when you were young
>
> your daughter's/son's performance on the playing field
>
> the crush on . . . you suffered from in the fourth grade
>
> a fantasy you had to: be on a TV talk show, make love to . . . play for the Bears, play the lead in . . .
>
> a dinner party that started out bad and . . .

# Chapter 17
# Including the Major Players

*I'll note you in my book of memory.*

—Henry IV, Part I, *William Shakespeare*

If your perverse imp is still whispering negative suggestions in your ear—such as wouldn't it be rather egotistical to write a story about *yourself?*—tell him to hush. No matter what the poets and sad songs say, none of us play our time upon the stage alone. Your memories are studded with significant people who have adorned, scarred, and skewed the plot of your life. Those you cherished and those who drove you crazy will be crucial ingredients in your narrative. You must summon back the men and women and children and animals who notably crossed your life. One of the major differences between a memoir and the proper autobiography: a memoir more often concerns itself with personalities and actions other than those of the writer herself, while an autobiography lays a heavier stress on the inner and private life of its author.

When novelist John Irving wrote a short memory about his first love, wrestling, he said, "An intractable phenomenon of writing a memoir is that you begin to miss the people you are writing about. I found myself wanting to call up people I hadn't seen or spoken to in more than thirty years."

The bank rents safe-deposit boxes for the title to your car, the deed to your house, the ruby ring you inherited from Aunt Myrtle, but to protect the important people you have known, put them in your stories before time, the worst thief, robs you of your impressions.

What made your father notable? Was he barrel-chested and bullheaded, a cup custard with a thin crusty skin, or, like mine, the greatest enigma you ever encountered?

Perhaps all you remember about that first real date is the agony and the awkwardness, like your stomach growling after you vowed you weren't hungry because you didn't want to eat and have him see your teeth looking disgusting. But there must have been someone on the other side of the table whose noble traits, at least, you could see. Did you like something about him, or was he simply the only person who asked? Was he nervous too? Maybe it is time to quiet your sister who is still saying your goofy taste in men began early.

After all this time, considering how suave you have become, it probably won't tarnish your image a bit to admit the first time a girl was finally willing to let you touch her breast, you couldn't manage the bra hooks, or her father turned on the porch light.

You might want to pay tribute to the first person who gave you a chance to prove yourself when you were about as qualified for the job/position as you were to make a lava-spitting volcano behave itself.

So it only lasted a week, but the short romance introduced you to tenderness you have tried to hold on to. Even though he probably will never read it, you might enjoy saying thank you for the memories.

Remember the time when you thought, If this is a dog-eat-dog world, then I need a Doberman to compete with John/Jane?

All the most beautiful girl in the world, whose name you no longer remember, did was add an extra scoop to the chocolate shake you ordered every afternoon at the local soda fountain, but she made you feel like a prince.

The mean-minded so-and-so you worked for in the eighties didn't make you feel like a prince. He tried to make you crawl on your belly. Attempting to recapture the feelings you had for them both could be an interesting trip back in time.

If it were a chance encounter, don't you often wonder why both of you had the good fortune/bad luck to take that plane/go to that bookstore/attend that concert at the same time? Dickens had to make up coincidences to keep his narratives flowing, but you could probably write several actual stories about pivotal people you have met through random encounters or flukes.

We lose contact, even with people who were once important. I love to read and to write stories about family, school, office-workers, reunions, where your memories can be reaffirmed or go into shock. Clarence, whom you remember as a nerd, now owns two city blocks in downtown Cleveland. Thomas is still the class flirt. The jock everyone predicted would play for the NBA could have been Updike's model for his character Rabbit—the basketball star who ended up selling Toyotas. Mary Elizabeth still makes you feel as if you are wearing a potato sack. The 1965 homecoming queen bought her reunion dress at Charisma. The girl you wanted to marry because she thought you were wonderful could now buy you out without depleting her savings account.

Funerals and weddings bring together people who surely deserve a chapter in your book of memories.

If we are to be judged by the company we keep, most of us could count on our friends not to portray us as heroes of the absurd, but there are exceptions. For a long time I've known someone I'll call Helen, who must be in charge. Sometimes she drives me nuts; other times I can laugh. The question is, What tone shall the narrator (I) take, and what impression, not only of my friend, but of me, do I want the reader to have? I could say I've put up with this dominating control freak, not because I'm a jerk, of course, but rather because I've been clever enough to outfox her. I could say, when I suggest we go to a movie, I always pick a flick I don't want to see and a day and time when I have other plans. Born to think of herself as the boss, Helen will have to reject my recommendation and propose one of her

own. Often she will pick the film and the day I actually
had in mind.

I admit I have tried this technique with Helen a couple
of times, but frankly it makes me feel (and appear in print)
manipulative and hasn't worked often enough to brag about
as I did above. Language like *put up with, dominating, control freak, jerk, outfox, flick, born to think of herself as the
boss,* has set a cynical tone bordering on sour.

Language reflects thought.

I have other options such as a condescending tone exag-
gerating Helen's quirks and my benevolent tolerance. Without stretching the truth, I could assume a cheerful voice
and present her as a lovable eccentric. A gentle, ironic tone
presenting either of us as naive could be humorous. My
computer usually shorts out at the suggestion of creating
a martyr role, but that is another possibility.

Memories aren't carved on some hard surface in our
brains. My remembrances of Helen are affected by moods.
When I eventually write about her, the portrait will be
shaped by how I am feeling about myself and the world at
large, just as the people in your story will be affected by
your outlook. In another chapter we will look further at the
malleability of our remembrances.

We are apt to change our minds about individuals, but
there are types who constantly plague us, like those who
have made our lives miserable because they "were only
doing their jobs." I could write a hundred thousand words
about steely-eyed state patrolmen with wired jaws and a
ticket quota to fill, especially those in Ohio where I know
they mass produce them in a factory behind the courthouse. And the bureaucrats who issue passports, driver's
licenses, and permits for doing things never meant to be
anyone else's business? Keep in mind I live in Manhattan,
but I have heard on good authority these people with the
blank faces and time clocks for hearts are imported daily
from the land of Nod.

Then there are the people who have outfoxed us. Anyone
who has ever played sports has a few stories about them.
My nephew Dannon had the body, but not the heart, for
competitive sports. His coaches said he lacked the killer
instinct. Having played in junior high with a ball hog who
disgusted him, Dannon had developed a habit of passing,

sometimes to the coach's horror, even when he had a good shot. He was playing varsity his sophomore year when the coach decided to break the pattern. It was the fourth quarter in a tight game against their strongest rival, when the coach sent them back on the floor with the instructions "No one shoots but Dannon." Dannon shot. The next morning we made an emergency appointment with the dermatologist. Overnight the kid's clear face had broken out in the most extreme case of acne the doctor had treated in some time.

There are those who deserve our ire. Invective is direct denunciation by using derogatory epithets, the kinds of things we say immediately after a reckless driver has smashed into our new car just as we are driving it away from the dealer's lot. I like Dryden's description of the difference in efficacy between direct depreciation by invective and the indirectness of irony in which the ironist is able to maintain the advantage of self-control and detachment by leaving it to circumstance to convert the bland accomplishments into insults:

> How easy it is to call rogue and villain, and that wittily. But how hard to make a man appear a fool, a blockhead, or a knave without using any of those opprobrious terms. . . . There is still a vast difference between the slovenly butchering of a man, and the fineness of a stroke that separates the head from the body, and leaves it standing in place.

What is your intent in portraying these people? is the question. You might as well think about it, because your tone will reveal it anyway. Remember, if revenge is your motive, the surgeon's cut is more artistic than the butcher's.

Gore Vidal reminds me of the troublemaking boys who got more of my attention than I intended when I taught high school English. Vidal's outrageous behavior in print provides so many blatant examples of the show-off, he receives more coverage than the writers I admire. His memoir suggests he has little admiration for anyone except himself and his first love Jimmie Trimble, who has been dead for fifty years. Either assuming or revealing an indifferent tone, Vidal claims to have once told a journalist, "I had

never wanted to meet most of the people that I had met,
and the fact that I never got to know most of them took
dedication and steadfastness on my part." Although he
states he deplores acts of "gratuitous cruelty," which he
attributes to E.M. Forster, he did get to know many famous
people well enough to separate their heads from the bodies
and leave them standing in place:

Mary McCarthy was "uncorrupted by compassion." Writing about having sex with Kerouac, he not only makes the
point he was on top, but also, "we both thought, even then,
that we owed it to literary history to couple." "Truman [Ca-
pote] thought his world was high society, never figured out
that the jet set was not high society. I was not about to let
him know."

But Vidal hones his knife to its sharpest for the family
known round the world. *New York Times* reviewer Christopher Lehmann-Haupt says if gratuitous cruelty is not the
motive, then "revenge is why Mr. Vidal writes so spitefully
about the Kennedy family, particularly his half sister's
stepsister, Jacqueline Kennedy Onassis, whom he calls
among other wicked things, 'selfish and self-aggrandizing
beyond the usual.' "

Still professing he doesn't give a fig about breaking with/
being dropped by the family, he says, "Between Bobby's
primitive religion and his family's ardent struggle ever up-
ward from Irish bog, he was more than usually skewed,
not at least by his own homosexual impulses, which Nure-
yev once told me, were very much in the air on at least
one occasion when they were together."

It is your call to determine if the name dropping is self-
aggrandizing or a shrewd way to increase sales of his memoir. The pleasure without the risks is one of the reasons
we like to read novels about characters who do and say
things we would never have the nerve to do.

Hemingway did not have a gnat-sized ego either, but he
never acquired Vidal's devilish, indifferent facade. My met-
aphorical image of Hemingway is of a boxer with his dukes
up, especially for those who might be competitors. Certainly his portrayal of Scott Fitzgerald in *A Moveable Feast*
hits below the belt. In the most disparaging incident, after
a rabbit punch to make sure the reader realizes Fitzgerald
drinks too much, has had limited sexual experience, and

Zelda—a male emasculator—has had a breakdown, Hemingway tells about Scott's doubting his own virility. Because he is such a good friend, Hemingway takes him to the men's room, checks him out, and says, "You're perfectly fine. . . . You look at yourself from above and you look foreshortened. Go over to the Louvre and look at the people in statues and then go home and look at yourself in the mirror in profile."

The skewed profile I find reflected in the mirror of that story is Hemingway's, but I could be prejudiced. I also admit to preferring Fitzgerald's stories about romantic young men who spiked the punch at Plaza tea dances to Hemingway's stoic soldiers, bullfighters, and hunters who were good at killing wherever they were.

Most of us are fortunate enough to have known people we admire, respect, and love, who will be central figures in our remembrances. Not often enough, but sometimes, we even find heroes. British novelist William Boyd immediately wrote a short memorial for *The New Yorker* about his relationship with Ken Saro-Wiwa, the Nigerian writer who was executed by his government. There will surely be more. I was serving on PEN's Freedom to Write Committee at the time of his death. Until the moment he was hanged, New York PEN members and staff, as well as organizations around the world, worked hard for his release. The last three days, never off the phone, the staff made a final, valiant effort especially to persuade Royal Dutch/Shell to save him. The other hope was Nelson Mandela's moral authority with the Nigerian leader General Abacha.

Boyd says, "We [international organizations] were baffled and confused, though, when Mandela did little more than persistently advocate that we should all be patient, that the problem would be resolved through an easy, low-key diplomacy."

Perhaps we should not have been baffled. Earlier in the year Mandela had published his autobiography, *Long Walk to Freedom*. The *New York Times* said: "On the evidence of his own version of his amazing life, the President of South Africa is no moralist or messiah but a pragmatic politician who always chose what might work over what was ideologically agreeable."

It seems to be difficult to hold on to one's hero stance if

one has to worry about winning elections. Mandela's advisers cautioned him against making a strong statement because of South Africa's business commitments to oil companies. The situation reminded me of Houseman's poem, "To an Athlete Dying Young." The poet says a lad is smart to slip away from fields "where glory does not stay," but rather "withers quicker than the rose."

If you have known someone admirable, whose laurel did not wither, including her in your memoir would be a fine tribute.

Then there was Theodfora Pozak, who must have had memories of his own, but preferred to make up *The Memoirs of Elizabeth Frankenstein,* a woman who had a famous brother. Pozak might have gotten his idea from Virginia Woolf, who also made up a sad tale about a young woman named Judith, who came to London to try her luck on the stage but did not have the success of her brother William Shakespeare.

With all of the people waiting in the wings of your memoir, I doubt you will have to make up characters. Perhaps some of the following exercises will help you determine whom to include.

## INCLUDING THE MAJOR PLAYERS

☞ The memory of him lingers on like a dry cough.

☞ She wasn't a liar, but she had the ability to put a spin on things, like listening to her tell about a party was more fun than attending.

☞ He was the dullest man I ever met. He wasn't interested in anything outside himself.

☞ Trouble was the backbone of the bittersweet relationship I had with her.

☞ He took a shortcut to the American Dream.

☞ She was disgustingly nice.

☞ "I'm a loner," . . . always said. "You're not supposed to be able to depend on a loner." How convenient, I thought.

☞ I should have sent her a recording of "Lady Be Good."

☞ I admired him because . . .

☞ I married . . . because.

☞ At times I actually wondered if they could have switched babies on us at the hospital.

☞ She didn't like sex.

☞ Somehow the folks back home never found out about . . .

☞ Conversation should be a concert with everyone drawn in, but with . . . it's always a solo.

☞ If God keeps a ledger . . .

☞ He had an intellectual sophistication and a knowing air of judgment, often mistaken for wisdom.

☞ The judge changed my life.

☞ . . . was the one who demanded the most from me.

☞ . . . was an imposter, but I didn't realize it in the beginning.

☞ . . . taught me love is action, not words.

☞ . . . lacked an identity. She would be whatever you wanted her to be.

☞ . . . eventually forgave me.

# Chapter 18
# Including the Major Places

*In contemporary America, where we come from is rarely our ultimate destination.*

—*"Home," Michael Dorris*

Even if he has a fine education, similar philosophies and goals in life, a man from Hope, Arkansas, cannot be like a man born in Boston, Massachusetts, any more than the Bostonian can be like a man raised in Hyde Park, New York. And a man can wear cowboy boots stained with oil and swear his favorite food is hog rinds, but East Coast preppies, not Texans, step in "deep do-do."

Earlier, I said we pass for who we are. We can polish and spit-shine our back stories, but eventually we also pass for where we came from, so it is best to put our birth certificates on the table at the start.

The day I, the first in my family, left for college, my father led me to the window of his office in an old livery stable with pegged, hand-hewn beams where he sold the shiniest orange Allis Chalmer tractors. It was fall, harvest time. He pointed to the prairie fields dotted with farmers picking beans, shucking corn. "If you ever get to thinking you have nothing in common with them, remember, they are sending you to school," my father said. I never have, but it was years before I realized he might have been asking me not to desert him. As if I ever could . . .

My father was a man who didn't travel, but he has followed me everywhere. When I was little, I used to ask him where we came from. "Fayette County," he always said. "But before that?" "The Willetts have always been in Fayette County, and if you have any sense, you'll stay here too," he replied. On my first trip to London, from the moment I got off the plane, I kept seeing these signs—WILLETT REAL ESTATE—and at Westminster Abbey a brass plaque indicated an old boy named Willett had donated a wing. I called my father. "Daddy, I think we might have come from England; there are—" "No, we've always been in Illinois. When are you coming home?"

I married a man from Illinois, but he didn't even know you had to mount a horse on his downtown side. I didn't even know an el was a train. His family had proudly lived in Mayor Daley's neighborhood. My father had told me Daley had horns just like FDR. Daddy had heard it from Everett Dirkson. Right outside Chicago there's a place called Illinois.

The part of the country where you grew up can be a shaping element in your story, as Brooklyn was for Kazin and Whitman, Concord for Thoreau, Dublin for Joyce, and a small Arkansas town has been for Maya Angelou.

Filming a show for public television some time ago, Bill Moyers and Angelou went back to her hometown. They were walking comfortably along a road talking, when they came to either a creek or a river. Suddenly Angelou reminded me of a horse who senses danger. Flooded with memories from the past, she stopped abruptly and didn't want to cross over the bridge that had segregated the black and white sides of town in her childhood. Moyers, with his soothing voice, finally talked her across and the show went on. Just as I don't recall if it were a creek or a river, I don't remember anything else about the program, just the bridge, the symbolic bridge that had been an important element in the making of a poet.

A memoir defining where you call home might be the most fascinating story of all, for you and your reader. Michael Dorris spent his youth crisscrossing America with his mother "in pursuit of our next stop." He and his wife, writer Louise Erdrich, found a home in New Hampshire in an old house that has a cracked foundation, floors that slope, yellowed newspapers for insulation. Dorris maintains our sense of home is a mental state of relative contentment, where we don't pine to be anywhere else, where we don't feel out of place or a stranger.

For some, "a new home" might be the ultimate oxymoron.

Half a dozen people I know could talk for a week, maybe write a book, about *1218 Madison Park,* that South Side address we once shared in enormous apartments not nearly large enough to contain our callow aspirations, hope, and energy. Lake Michigan splashes the edge of Hyde Park, home of the University of Chicago, a short el ride from the Loop—a community whose prosperity has risen and fallen with the tides of social change. Once—in the days of Leopold and Loeb—grand enough for the doges of Venice, the neighborhood went down. Mansions with ballrooms became boardinghouses. Crime stalked the streets. Then academics, artists, social liberals, blazed a renaissance.

With friends, we co-opted a classic Chicago building, three stories of railroad flats, but this was one heck of a long train, slightly derailed by neglect. In its day, a governor had designed our apartment to accommodate a cocktail party for five hundred. The butler's pantry—one of three—was twice the size of my New York kitchen. My father, who thought we were mad, lent us some money. When he came to inspect his investment, he paced off the size as he would have an acre of land.

Laid out around a long, oval green like an English muse, the friendly houses and apartment buildings in Madison Park looked each other in the eye. Sometimes late at night an unidentified man in a kilt played a bagpipe out there in the dark park. In the sunlight, kids of all colors knocked each other down, held Easter egg hunts. Adults of all ages held rallies for McGovern, Abner Mikva, and peace. Bill Mauldin, Louis Farrakhan, lived in big houses down the street.

We got our degrees, we got transferred, we got divorced.

We discarded our innocence, like yesterday's clothes, and set out to make our marks around the world . . . in less space.

"Some of you will go and some of you will stay" is often the refrain in commencement speeches. Thinking about where you came from, where you are, why you never left, the effect places have had on shaping who you have become, could be the most challenging aspect of your memoir. Shifting the spotlight from you to the setting is another way to tell your story without sounding like a megalomaniac.

*Midnight in the Garden of Good and Evil,* John Brendt's memoir about his fascination with the party town Savannah, Georgia, became a best-seller. The success of such an unlikely subject would have been enough to give a lesser man delusions of grandeur, but Brendt doesn't appear to be the type. His writing style was to keep the stage lights directed on Savannah, Conrad Aiken's hometown. Aiken's father shot his mother and then himself. Why? Parties. She went to too many, gave too many. As he drank martinis poured from a silver shaker by a silver-haired grand dame, Brendt received his first Savannah history lesson sitting on Aiken's gravestone. At the end of the writer's life, he had returned to Savannah and spent much of his time watching the ships. His marker is a bench overlooking the harbor with the inscription COSMOS MARINER, DESTINATION UNKNOWN.

Purposely isolated, there are no direct routes to Savannah, the old South, where Gucci carpetbaggers, big business, and superhighways are not welcome. Brendt had a difficult time getting there on a zigzagging route from Charleston. He had a harder time getting away. Coming for a weekend, he ended up spending much of the next eight years in this hauntingly beautiful city of moss-hung oaks and shaded squares. He met the well-bred society ladies, a young redneck gigolo, a black drag queen, learned about the infamous murder case involving people at Mercer House, the mansion where the movie *Glory* was shot, Johnny Mercer grew up, and which Jackie Onassis offered to buy for two million dollars. Although the story is as spellbinding as a mystery novel, it is Brendt's memoir in which the main character is an arrogant, beautiful city.

Savannah is especially exotic, but changing our address—no matter where it is—affects our senses. Moving to any city from a farm or small town shocks the system. Some cities have such powerful personalities, they can actually change ours. If you have doubts, think about what has happened to people you have helped send to Washington, D.C.

For some of us, the geographic change is like being born again, especially in cities that have characters as distinct as our friends. Chicago is an optimistic city, always has been. Sinclair Lewis cynically called it boosterism, but I liked living there, where people thought things were going to get better and they usually did. San Francisco, New Orleans, Boston, New York, London, Venice, Vancouver, have also inspired the poet in us to sing.

For others the pace, the crowds, the litter, the alienation, the crime, torment like purgatory if not hell. E.B. White, who gave up on the city and moved to a farm in Maine, said in *Here Is New York:*

> Of any person who desires such queer prizes, New York will bestow the gift of loneliness and the gift of privacy. It is this largess that accounts for the presence within the city's walls of a considerable section of the population; for the residents of Manhattan are to a large extent strangers who have pulled up stakes somewhere and come to town, seeking sanctuary or fulfillment or some greater or lesser grail. The capacity to make such dubious gifts is a mysterious quality of New York. It can destroy an individual, or it can fulfill him, depending a good deal on luck. No one should come to New York to live unless he is willing to be lucky.

My friend Rosemary is willing to be lucky. She claims shopping as her major sport and New York as her major playing field. When she turns up at lunch looking like a billion bucks in a couture outfit she found at a sample sale for a song, I want to burn what I'm wearing and sue the store where I paid retail. Every woman I know would read Rosemary's memoir, if she would write *My Secrets of Seventh Avenue Showrooms.*

Driving down Seventh Avenue with all of the pushcarts, delivery trucks, brazen young men pushing racks of fur coats right down the middle of the street, can be a nightmare unless you're doing research on how to cuss someone out in seven languages. But beyond those grimy doorways, up those creaky elevators, to glitz, glamour, and the grand, now there's a setting for a story.

Rosemary now commutes to shopping sprees, however. She has moved to Litchfield, Connecticut, an elegant old village where bargains would be considered déclassé. Litchfield real estate tends to go for eight figures, a pound of cheese or pâté can cost more than a pair of blue jeans, but every house has a history, some have ghosts, and gossip clings to many iron gates. I can imagine a memoir with a Litchfield mansion as a main character.

Have you spent four hours per day commuting to the city so you and your kids could walk barefooted on green grass? Or do you think kids who have too much grass and too few museums are culturally deprived? A commuter's memoir could be interesting. I would read something like *Thirty-five Years of Adventures on the 7:02.*

If you were a suburban kid, you might have spent more time in the mall than in the yard. I have prowled the Iowa malls with Dannon. They remind me of fun houses. I can never remember where we came in and fear there is no way out.

Mark Salzman wrote *Lost in Place: Growing Up Absurd in Suburbia,* a refreshing memoir of a teenager's search for happiness through kung fu in the 1970s. Salzman knows how to write with a twinkle in his eye. Most of the jokes are on him.

Think of the trips you have taken to faraway places and across town. Maybe you had to kiss the Blarney stone before you gave a hoot about Parnell, hear a chant in an African village before you stopped processing your hair. Many vows to mend wicked ways have been made at the Western Wall, which has also been called the Wailing Wall. Jews make pilgrimages to Israel and find their roots in a country that came into existence after they were born. How has a sense of place affected you in your travels or in the house you call home?

Geminis are allowed two natures, but I have at least three, maybe four. In Maine my moods change with the tide, the weather, the sun's rising and setting. Having to go into town when the surf crashes against the rocks is a sacrifice. Coming back to the island, aware of what I'm

missing, I always drive too fast. Even on deadline days I
have lost hours daydreaming, watching the ocean change
colors, a lobsterman hauling his traps, a freighter heading
for ports unknown.

In New York I have resented missing a space in a revolv-
ing door. My heart starts beating faster by the time the
cab crosses the Fifty-ninth Street Bridge. My typing speed
increases. I sprint down the streets, dodging people.

At "home" in Vandalia, Illinois, it can take an hour to
walk a block. I stop to chat with a neighbor who has had
an operation, a farmer who has a story about my father,
one of my mother's friends from the church who will bake
me a gooseberry pie, to flirt with an old boyfriend who is
still kind of cute, or gossip with a Hi-Gal who knows all
the news.

When I travel, I try to become a chameleon, except in
California.

If people live on seaweed, fill their cereal bowls with vita-
min pills, dye their hair mulberry, pierce their nipples, join
the John Birch Society, or believe in reincarnation, Ronald
Reagan's trickle-down theory, or Mickey Mouse, "Oh,
they're from California," is explanation enough.

If you are from California, I would bet the farm on not
having to suggest you include the setting in your memoir.
My friend David used to begin every telephone conversation
with "Hi, this is Dave, just checking in from Paradise."

Some states get a worse rap than they deserve. Before I
had ever been there, I remember being horrified to learn
Princeton was in New Jersey.

Geography might not be important in your story, but
maybe a building, a room, a garden, plays an important
role. As a teenager, I used to park on Thrill Hill with a
freckle-faced basketball player named Skippy. Perhaps for
you a hospital room began to remind you of a cage, a win-
dowless office felt like a torture chamber, a high-rise apartment complex housed no friendly faces. I no longer
remember where I read it, but I can't forget a writer's saying the sounds coming from his parents' bedroom made it
sound like a torture chamber.

I address letters to my friend John: "Hooterville International Airport." Hooterville, a grassy strip on his farm in
Illinois, was so named by its original owner, Red Irving, a

spunky stunt pilot—who, among other flamboyant tricks, used to land his open cockpit plane on moving railroad flatcars. John's illustrious ancestors can be traced back to Lincoln's cabinet, but the memoir John works on is framed by Hooterville and the flashy barnstormer who planted a runway in his cornfield.

Settings can have symbolic significance. When I served on the board of trustees for a university, a generous donor gave money for a chapel. Thanking the man, the president said the chapel was what the school needed, "a place to get in out of the wind."

The following exercises might help you to remember a place that deserves to be included in your story.

## INCLUDING THE MAJOR PLACES

- ☞ The place you think of as home
- ☞ The most frightening place you've ever been
- ☞ Christmas morning
- ☞ Sailing in a storm
- ☞ A house you hated
- ☞ A picnic
- ☞ A dinner party where diplomacy was called for
- ☞ Your teenage hangout
- ☞ The boss's office
- ☞ Camp when you were ten
- ☞ The locker room
- ☞ Your stateroom
- ☞ A sickroom
- ☞ The fraternity/sorority house
- ☞ A country that did not welcome tourists
- ☞ A city laid out with no logical plan
- ☞ A city remembered for its smells

- ☞ The view from your hotel window
- ☞ It wasn't a fancy restaurant, but it was your place
- ☞ They said it was haunted
- ☞ You went there when you needed to escape
- ☞ You lost it in the divorce settlement
- ☞ A place that had shrunk in your imagination
- ☞ A place never intended for a woman in high heels
- ☞ The travel agent had promised it would be exotic
- ☞ The church where you were married
- ☞ A summer cottage on the lake
- ☞ The farm in winter
- ☞ The swimming hole
- ☞ The casino
- ☞ The street as it was waking up
- ☞ The street at night when the lights went on

# WRITING YOUR MEMOIR

*This is the use of memory*
*For liberation—not less of love but expanding*
*Of love beyond desire and so liberation*
*From the future as well as the past.*

*—"Four Quartets," T.S. Eliot*

# Chapter 19
# Myth and Memory:
# Reinventing, Reconstructing,
# Reordering

*We tell ourselves stories to live.*

—*Joan Didion*

As Dylan Thomas said, "I can never remember whether it snowed for six days and six nights when I was twelve or whether it snowed for twelve days and twelve nights when I was six."

The summer I was eighteen, my mother suggested we go back to the farm where I was born. This was after a visit by some of my college friends, at which time I had told stories about the farm—how, in the first grade, I had to walk three miles to school, how our lane was a mile from the main road. My friends had been impressed. When we turned down the lane to the farm, I was driving. I slammed on the brakes, pitching Mother and me into the windshield. "What happened?" Mother smiled as I covered my face, before looking again. At best, the lane might have been a long city block. The school might have been a mile away, if we had gone down the road, but Vivian and Gene, the kids I walked with, lived across the road and we always cut through their pasture.

Once—for about a week in my wild, impetuous youth—I was engaged to a Park Avenue expatriate who ran a bar on Mallorca. I remember how he reminded me of Lord Byron and how his eyes looked as if he had a mysterious past. I hope I never see him again. He was the most handsome man I ever knew.

Even Ovid frequently remarked, "so it is believed."

Jackie Kennedy Onassis once told *New York Times* reporter Francesca Stanfill that when you look back on your life, you hardly recognize the person you once were. Like a snake shedding skins. Stanfill said Onassis had shed several. I think the reporter is right. Even though the lovely features are similar, the images I have of Jackie Bouvier, Jackie Kennedy, Jackie Onassis, and finally "Jackie," are of different people. Stanfill suggested she was a passive observer of her own myth and the shrewdest politician this century has ever seen, able to transform "unseemliness by imaginatively re-creating the past into her version of the truth." Stanfill reported a close friend saying Jackie would not speak of things she found disagreeable. For instance, she said nothing about Onassis's death for months. When she finally spoke, she reminisced warmly about her marriage to him, describing a marriage that did not exist and an affection that was not there, just as she never spoke about John Kennedy's infidelity or her father's difficulty with alcohol.

In the *Iliad*, Homer softened the rude barbaric nature of his characters.

When we turn reality into myth, we aren't necessarily lying. George Vaillant said once a caterpillar becomes a butterfly, it doesn't remember being a caterpillar.

Memories do not travel through time alone. Imagination is a constant companion. Most of us, unable to drag around Emerson's "monstrous corpse of memory," reinvent the past to make the thought of it endurable. William Zinsser, my colleague at The New School, defines *memoir* as the art of inventing the truth.

Holocaust survivor Elie Wiesel has devoted his life to trying to make certain people don't forget or reinvent the truth about the Nazi atrocities. In his latest memoir, *All Rivers Run to the Sea,* he said:

> Memory is a passion no less powerful or pervasive than love. What does it mean to remember? It is to live in more than one world, to prevent the past from fading and to call upon the future to illuminate it. It is to revive fragments of existence, to rescue lost beings, to cast harsh light on faces and events, to drive back the sands that cover the surface of things to combat oblivion and to reject death.

Viewing memory as having a transformative, reconstructive power is not a theory Freud and his followers would have approved. Freud must have pictured the brain like a computer with an enormous storage capacity. He believed all autobiographical experience had been stored and could be recalled by therapy, hypnosis, interrogation, drugs, or meditation, just as a computer file can be reclaimed in its exact form if we can find the right command. If this were true, I imagine we would be building mental hospitals at the same rate we build prisons.

The view of memory as a transformative, reconstructive power is one increasingly shared by many researchers. Psychology professor John Cadre believes memories are more malleable and subject to revision. In *White Gloves: How We Create Ourselves Through Memory,* he says, "Memories don't sit inertly in our minds the way they do on an audiotape or the shelves of a library. They are constantly refashioned."

Cadre believes memories are transformed by new information, by suggestions received from others, and by shifts in one's own emotional needs at different times.

> On one hand, it [the remembering self] has the temperament of a librarian, a keeper of memory's most important archives. It can be fastidious in that role, guarding its original records and trying to keep them pristine . . . but memory's archivist by day has a secret passion by night: to fashion a story about itself, a story that some of us call the personal myth . . . not a falsehood but a comprehensive view of reality. . . . [This refashioned reality] speaks to the heart as well as the mind, seeking to generate conviction about what

it thinks is true. . . . As a maker of myth, the self leaves its handiwork everywhere in memory. With the passing of time, the good guys in our lives get a little better and the bad guys a little worse. The speeds get faster, the Depression gets tougher.


Norman Maclean, the teacher and colleague I admired most at the University of Chicago, was also my next-door neighbor in Madison Park. When he published his much-acclaimed *A River Runs Through It* as fiction, I was surprised. These were the boyhood stories he had told me around the dinner table. In the introduction he explains how the book grew from memoir to fiction:

"As is known to any teller of stories who eventually tries to put a few of them down in writing, the act of writing changes them greatly, so none of these stories closely resemble any story I ever told my children. For one thing, writing makes everything bigger and longer."

Willie Turner left a 486-page memoir. Of course, he had time to make his bigger and longer. Turner—known as a jailhouse Houdini—spent the last fifteen years of his life on death row. The first line of his story may be the most honest—"I was born into a world of sho 'nuff hard times back in December 9, 1945"—but his last word confirms his right to be known as the "Genius of Death Row." The night he died, as he had requested, his lawyer took his typewriter apart. He found a note with one word, "Smile." In a cut-out hiding slot the lawyer also found a working .32-caliber Smith & Wesson revolver, a bag of bullets, and two small saw blades, an escape artist's staple. So Willie Turner, who had broken out of more prisons than most of us have ever seen, had the last laugh. Near the end he had often said, "I'm *letting* them do this to me."

Turner's typewriter still worked, by the way. His version of the murder that sent him to death row doesn't fit eyewitness accounts, but the humiliating story of sending his girlfriend a father's Valentine because he was illiterate has been confirmed. At twenty-eight, Turner not only learned to read and write in prison, but also to draw so he could apply for a patent for a barber tool he had invented. Prisoners couldn't have rulers, but he made do with a hacksaw blade, which he also used to fashion a piece of plastic into a drawing compass. U.S. Patent No. 4,428,119, he wrote, was the first token of legitimate respect he had ever received.

When Turner was executed in 1995, his memoir had not been published. In a *New Yorker* piece, "The Genius of Death Row," Peter J. Boyer said, "It is a long, rambling memoir of questionable factual accuracy, as might be expected of a master con's effort to explain away a life of violence and crime." However, Caroline Schloss, the psychologist for Correctional Medical Services who quit her job after falling in love with Turner, still has hopes of finding a publisher.

Several of my New York friends see psychologists or psychiatrists, and one goes to gurus and psychics. Even though none of them have found anyone with the commitment of Caroline Schloss, I have collected a lot of secondhand information free of charge. Since life "ain't been no crystal stair" for anyone I know, as long as it's legal, I usually support anything that makes the climb easier. Yet my head begins to spin when the same friends who used to tell me funny, ironic, affectionate stories about their families begin to talk about fathers who sexually abused them, or insensitive, nonsupportive parents who pressured them into marriage, which explains why they did not have a successful career or marriage. So often I hear, "I didn't even remember until my analyst said I had patterns of behavior suggesting I had been sexually abused." In fiction when the storyteller's information comes from an unconfirmed source, we label him an unreliable narrator. Still, I can understand why answers to problems we don't understand can be consoling. Often these retrieved wrongs can then be used to explain or excuse most botched endeavors. Failure, letting ourselves down, is hard to handle. The need for comfort, the need to stay balanced, is why we have defensive mechanisms.

Fortunately, the people I know work out their problems privately with their analysts or a few trusted friends. Then there are those who do it publicly and charge us for the privilege. Buy one of Philip Roth's later novels or go to a Woody Allen film. When Allen breaks a woman's heart or takes up with a young girl not even half his age, he boldly parades his justifications in films for the whole world. After seeing one of his films, a *New York Times* op-ed reporter once said Allen had been shrunk until he had no conscience, and at a certain age even Cary Grant had the good taste to stop kissing ingenues.

My imagination has always acted like an unbridled racehorse without being fed by anyone else. Suggested memory concerns me. My opinion and a token will take you to Brooklyn, but if I were a judge, I wouldn't allow it as admissible evidence.

Another view for the origins of the stories we tell orginated with psychologist C.G. Jung. He believed our narratives come from primordial images formed by repeated experiences in the lives of our ancestors, inherited in the "collective unconscious" of the human race. His view explains the archetypal characters, images, and plot patterns that recur frequently in the stories we tell each other. The death-rebirth theme is said to be the basic archetype, and images of the Fatal Woman, the ruthless Male Hero, the Devil and God, some of the prototypical characters. The profound emotional response to tales like Faulkner's *The Sound and The Fury* happens because it resonates with an image already existing in the unconscious mind.

Faulkner, like T.S. Eliot, devoted himself consciously and unconsciously to a world defeated by its excesses. His works that dredge deep in the subconscious, especially *The Sound and The Fury*, celebrate the grandeur of destruction. The land and the landowners are accursed, he indicates, by having profited from slavery, by yielding to the money-ridden evils of Reconstruction, and by coddling the remnants of an aristocracy that has lost courage and honor. Faulkner wrote fiction, but the essence of many of the characters can be traced to members of his own family, like Colonel Sartoris, based on Faulkner's great-grandfather, the last of the Faulkner aristocrats.

As I work on this manuscript, sixty-five years after Faulkner published *The Sound and The Fury*, the morning newspaper headlines boldly proclaim the sins of the rich and powerful, and warn of racial unrest, greed, and the loss of a social conscience.

As you work on your memoir, you could have surprises in store. My Maine artist friend, Marlene, now laughs about the years of her life taken over by Taava Miina Kallioniemi

Ekola, her potent Finnish grandmother, an Upper Peninsula immigrant and a healer who became the stuff of myth and legend. Marlene's Michigan childhood was filled with the stories, and Taava Miina, who was not about to be forgotten, traveled with her in her memory and imagination when she left. Gradually Taava Miina became the artist's muse. Not only a collection of visual art, but a corpus of poems, were the result. "First a shred of memory will come into my awareness," Marlene says, "or something out of a dream, or perhaps a letter will trigger my thinking and a poem will result."

Until I began to read Jung, I worried about "arrested development." It was this cowboy fetish. I thought Belle Starr, lady outlaw—leader of the Younger gang—might have been a healthy persona for a kid with a horse, but for an educated New York woman with silver in her hair, for pity's sake? The silver pistols with red plastic handles are long gone, but I still wear jeans and cowboy boots and feel the holsters on my hips.

When I used to ride Prince down the alleys of our village, shooting wonderfully noisy caps at my pursuers, I liked to scare Rose Haley to death. Rose had never heard of being politically correct, but even then she told Mother there was no such thing as a toy gun. Mother told me my Scottish ancestors, who settled in Montana and became cowboys, ranched and rode the rodeo. They didn't shoot anyone. Most of those cowboys were dead before my mother was born, and I certainly never met any of them, but I think I have their stride and a bit of their hearts. When Pam Houston wrote *Cowboys Are My Weakness*, I felt as if she had written her stories to preserve my memories.

There are many examples of writers who have literally written to save their lives. At a desperate time in his life, Scott Fitzgerald is alleged to have said he wrote *The Crack Up* to keep from doing so. More recently, Susanna Kaysen's powerful memoir, *Girl, Interrupted*, is an attempt to make sense of nearly two years she spent at the famed McLean psychiatric hospital, where Robert Lowell and Sylvia Plath had been treated. Lowell's *Life Studies* includes McLean experience poems like "Walking in the Blue" and "Home After Three Months Away."

Whether you tap into the blocked-off residue of your

past, the collective unconscious of the human race, or explore the jumble of memories surrounding the Christmas when you were ten, I predict the experience will enrich your life. Tell it the way it was, or at least the way you remember it.

Maureen Dowd turned off her cynical voice when she wrote a column about trying unsuccessfully to throw things away when she was moving on to another stage, a new place to live. She decided: "Clutter is beautiful. It is the stuff of memory, the evidence of an unexamined life that is worth living."

Dig into the clutter of your memories. Now is the time for all good men *and* women to . . . WRITE.

# Chapter 20
# Focusing

*In her singular memoir,* People Who
Led to My Plays, *Adrienne
Kennedy unpacks her life like an
orderly woman laying out the
contents of a suitcase after an
arduous journey.*

—*Ben Brantley,* New York Times
*drama critic*

I always hate the opening of autobiographies where you
have to find out who everyone's grandfather was and what
he did for a living.

Unlike an autobiography, where you are expected to
begin at the beginning, a memoir gives you the freedom to
start at the best part.

Don't think you must summarize your life before you
arrive at the point you want to emphasize. A memoir is a
window into a portion of your experience at a particular
time in a specific place with certain people. Think narrow.
You are about to become the editor of your own life, imposing on an untidy sprawl a narrative shape and an organizing
idea. An author will sometimes announce his intentions in

**117**

the title as did Spiro T. Agnew, the vice president to Richard Nixon, who was forced to resign. His bold title, *Go Quietly . . . Or Else* serves as a headline for the reader and a structuring device for Agnew.

The power in good memoirs comes, not from how much they cover, but from the narrowness of their focus and the richness of the details. It is an act of writing frozen in a unique period—A Berkeley Flower Child in the Sixties, A Seabee on Normandy, The Fifties in Flint, Carrying Papers in Peoria. I like Zinsser's comment that unlike autobiography, which spans an entire life, a memoir assumes the life and ignores almost all of it. Actually, I can't think of any of the man's insights on writing with which I disagree.

I suggest you forget the image of your red contorted face screaming in protest from the doctor's slap and the difficulty of getting born. I know Wordsworth believed we enter life "not in utter nakedness, But trailing clouds of glory," however, if you think you remember the delivery room, it is probably a phantom memory. Someone else has more than likely planted the recollections in your mind.

Shirley MacLaine, the Joyce Carol Oates of memoirs, can get anywhere from here, back in time, into the future, but she is at her best when she stays put in Hollywood, writing movingly about her love affair with Robert Mitchum, who "saw himself as a common stiff, born to be lonely," expecting "nothing from life except that the roof doesn't leak."

Think of your life as an enormous two-dimensional mural wrapping around your study. The colors might be cloudy or faded, the images blurred and hazy. Keep looking until you find the more colorful spots—where the people, the places, the scenes, are at least in bas-relief. You will be able to plump them up. Perhaps they have begun to emerge in the practice exercises, you have had a dream, or out of the blue, shards of a past experience have begun to interrupt your thoughts. If you are lucky, your head is full of memories you have always wanted to preserve from childhood, the four years you played varsity ball, your experience as a young mother, your first job, or your time in the army. Put a frame around that particular place in time.

I would read anyone's version of "The First Time I Saw the Person I Was to Marry." We will use it as an example of where to start. Unless he was somehow involved in the meeting, like being a marriage broker, there is no reason to talk about your grandfather and what he did for a living.

Focus on what is inside the frame: you, your spouse-to-be, the time and place, the circumstances, and your feelings—his if they showed. The frame will impose unity on your piece, keep you from meandering away to unrelated incidents. The narrow fix makes your story easier to structure. Think of the frame being the viewing window on your camera:

- ☞ What do you see?
- ☞ Where are you? Do you hear street sounds, the surf, the approaching subway?
- ☞ Is it winter?
- ☞ How old are you?
- ☞ Does it matter what you are wearing?
- ☞ Is music playing? Was it the Jefferson Airplane, Hank Williams, Frank Sinatra, or Pavarotti?
- ☞ What does your spouse-to-be look like? Did he have hair then?
- ☞ Is he sure of himself? Are you?
- ☞ What does he say?
- ☞ Were you shocked/delighted/impressed/angry?
- ☞ How does he behave? How do you respond?
- ☞ Does a gesture give him away? You?
- ☞ What happens?
- ☞ Is there anything in the frame that was there all the time, but you couldn't see at the time?

Looking back on that picture, how do you feel about it: amused, detached, ironic, cynical, nostalgic? As you recall from a previous chapter, your attitude toward the subject will set the tone. Before you write a word, decide what point of view you, the narrator, will assume. The voice should be consistent from beginning to end. "Jake had a loser's slouchy walk, even at eighteen" reveals one opinion, while "The convertible wasn't even white, but the first time I saw Jake swing his long legs right over the door, I heard the clank of chain mail" raises a quite different expectation.

Before Caitlin Thomas looked back at her life with Dylan, most people already knew the tempestuous nature of their relationship from news stories and gossip columns. After enough time had passed for her to gain some perspective, she wrote a second book about their life together. Able now to see beyond her anger and grief, she said she realized it was a love story, a very sad one, but nevertheless a love story. She set a different tone in *CAITLIN, Life with Dylan Thomas.* Her straightforward first line is: "Dylan told me that he loved me the very first night we met. . . ."

You establish your voice in the first line. You will lose your reader if you are coy, apologetic, phony, boastful, and—for this reader, the worst of all—whiny. Who wants to spend page and page with Pitiful Pearl?

Whether you love or hate what you see inside that frame, it is crammed with details only you can see. The next decision is where to begin and where to stop.

## BEGINNINGS AND ENDINGS

A reader has a subconscious need for order. Your story should be like a road map with a starting point leading to the destination without your audience having to stop to figure out where in the devil you are taking them.

If you write your first piece in one draft, expect wise men bearing mirth. The most polished professional doesn't dash off finished copy in her first version. She will usually have to sharpen, tighten, change the lead, or even start over.

I belong to the school that says when the words and ideas are running, get them all down before they swim away.

Read what you have written aloud. When you come to the interesting part, you have found your beginning. You will discover the story does not always begin where you began to write. Punching the delete button takes courage. When you have found the snappy line that should be the starting point, perhaps you simply reposition it. If that doesn't work, be brave. Cut out what goes before.

Remember you are telling a story, not explaining an incident, making a speech, or giving a lecture. If what you really want to do is warn women about being swayed by handsome men, that is a different forum. Stories dramatize the action, reveal character, and most important, you show the reader the scene and let him decide how he feels about it rather than telling him what to think. More about developing the "show, don't tell" technique later.

Beware beginning with a breezy generalization like: "Every woman likes handsome men, and I am no exception."

Even worse is opening with an insincere question such as "Did you ever fall in love at first sight with someone four inches shorter than you, who, as it turns out, was already engaged to your first cousin?" No, I never did, not that you give a fig about my answer, and since you have already summarized your experience in the first line, I have lost interest in reading about yours.

Granted, falling in love is mysterious, but attempting to turn it into a phony thriller would also be a mistake. "It was midnight. I was the only passenger in the last car on the dark train. As lightning flashed through the window, I felt his presence. IT HAPPENED SO QUICKLY." The *IT* and the capitals is a false suspense signal. Holding back information is only justified if a series of events builds to the resolution of a mystery.

The lead, the hook, the grabber, that omnipotent first sentence, make all the difference in your memoir. You're trying to seize the reader's attention, which doesn't mean you have to hit him broadside. You can charm with the freshness of your language, the liveliness of your voice. You can surprise him, arouse his curiosity, create tension as John Brendt does in the opening of *Midnight in the Garden of Good and Evil:*

> He was tall, about fifty, with darkly handsome, almost sinister features: a neatly trimmed mustache, hair turning silver at the temples, and eyes so black they were like the tinted windows of a sleek limousine—he could see out, but you couldn't see in.

When you have a starting point, decide the ending so you will know to stop when you get there. What impression do you want to leave? Since death is the only real ending for anyone's story, the last line, in some form or another, is always: "The end is only the beginning." I have always liked the title of Moss Hart's book, *Act One*, as well as the last line: "Not bad, kid," he would say. "Not a bad curtain for a first act." Unfortunately, Hart died while he was working on act two.

Read your first draft again. Is there a surprise, an interesting spot before you reach your original conclusion? How would it sound if you stopped there? Have you accomplished what you set out to do? Would you leave people wanting to know what happened next, or even better, having come to know the people so well, they could predict what would happen next?

Think about telephone conversations with the people who don't know how to say good-bye. They drive you as crazy as the guests who stand awkwardly at the door trying to say good night until you feel as if you have begun to sleepwalk. Remembrances that go on and on after you have said what you have to say will leave the same scintillating effect.

Making the following decisions will help you to corner that part of your past you wish to spotlight.

## FOCUSING

   ☞   The date

   ☞   The place

   ☞   The people involved

   ☞   The amount of time the incident will cover

   ☞   The cause

   ☞   The effect

   ☞   My attitude then

   ☞   My attitude now

# Chapter 21
# Creating a Setting to Be Felt and Seen

*Under the volcanoes, beside the snow-*
*capped mountains, among the*
*huge lakes, the fragrant, the silent,*
*the tangled Chilean forest . . . I*
*have come out of that landscape, that*
*mud, that silence to roam, to go*
*singing through the world.*

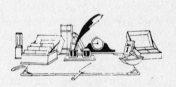

—*Pablo Neruda,* Memoirs

Thoreau said in his *Journal,* "We are as much as we see."
I would add, "and what we remember."

People and places provide the yeast in the dough for your
memoirs. You can punch them down or try to knead away
those experiences you would just as soon forget. But if you
say "I remember . . ." and that embarrassing experience in
boot camp or at a Jimi Hendrix concert in Cleveland rises
again and again, you might as well write it out of your
system. Places leave their mark.

Readers will gladly go with you to Cleveland or Cambo-
dia, into your dreams or back to your boyhood, as long as
they know where they are in time and place: "The Japanese
bombed Pearl Harbor when I was fourteen. I felt the shock
at a soda fountain in Des Moines, Iowa." "That summer
on Martha's Vineyard, it rained every day, or that's how I

remember it thirty years later." "My honeymoon wasn't
what it was cracked up to be, but Paris was."

Magazine editor and newspaper reporter Mary Cantwell
called her memoir *MANHATTAN, When I Was Young*, an-
nouncing in advance she would be sharing the billing with
the city. Cantwell came to town in her pageboy hairdo and
a cloud of Arpege, when New York was golden—a world of
white gloves, low rents, roomy checker cabs. It was also
the summer they executed the Rosenbergs and when Sylvia Plath first attempted suicide. Readers want to know
where and when as well as what and why. Putting your
story in historical context satisfies their need and helps
you to keep your focus.

For twenty-five years people have continued to suspend
disbelief to read Jack Finney's novel *Time and Again* in
which Si Morley steps out of his twentieth-century New
York apartment—right into the winter of 1882. Si is told:
"Sleep. And when you awake everything you know of the
twentieth century will be gone from your mind. Tonight is
January 21, 1882. There are no such things as automo-
biles, no planes, computers, television. 'Nuclear' appears
in no dictionary. You have never heard the name Richard
Nixon." Finney accomplishes his feat by re-creating 1882
with tangible details, like horse cars, el trains, the lobby
of the old Astor House, that allow the reader to see where
he is and when the scene is taking place.

Put a banner above your computer: MY OBLIGATION TO THE
READER IS TO SHOW TIME AND PLACE. You can begin your tale
in the present in Columbus, then move back to 1970 in
Canarsie, but unless you alert your audience to the switch
in time and place, they will feel abandoned in Columbus
and abandon you after a confusing paragraph or two. Time
and place transitions are bridges leading to a new setting,
another date: "My new boss reminds me of the pirate I
tried to be on All Saints' Night when my brother and I went
trick-or-treating in our Canarsie neighborhood. I must
have been seven or eight. . . ."

Now that you have taken us to Canarsie, let us see its
special qualities, smell the smells, hear the sounds, feel
the ambience. Write with all of your senses. Remember
how your nose tickled in a place like the deli that sold
briny dill pickles out of a barrel. Let the reader feel how

the sidewalk felt on bare feet when the temperature went over a hundred.

Frankly, I would find it easier to make Canarsie come alive than Venice or London. Sure, I gulped the first time I saw the canals, the gondolas, the Bridge of Sighs, Saint Mark's Square, Westminster Abbey, the Tower of London, Buckingham Palace . . . just as have a few hundred thousand other writers who have said "amazing," "astonishing," "another world," "sense of history." Leave the "land of mystery and adventure," "endless fascination lingering in the air," "exotic land," for the travel brochure writers. You could probably retire if friends and relatives had given you a dollar instead of writing a postcard from "where the old meets the new" or the place that has "a sense of old-world charm."

Clichés work like hit men, sneaking in when you're not looking to shoot down your story. Become a sleuth. Root them out before they do their dirty work.

Take the reader someplace he has probably never been, a secret place you have only showed to special people.

Unless you grew up on the river, I'd wager you've never walked across a swinging bridge, clutching the rope side rails as the narrow floorboards, resting on chain fencing, swayed under your tennis shoes high above swift waters overflowing its banks.

Our river forked around a good-sized island covered with rich topsoil dumped by the floods that always came. In the spring before the rains, farmers took their machinery over the old iron bridge on the west side of the island and left it in the fields, but that was the long way round—a twenty-five-mile trip, one way. No one could remember who had first looped the ingenious foot bridge between two huge oak trees. The faint of heart said crossing it was suicidal. Those ruled by common sense, like my father, said it saved gas. He and I had an unofficial contract. He let me do dangerous things like ride horses that bucked, ride on the fender of the truck, ride on top of a combine's tall grain bin, or drive the pickup with the choke pulled out before I could reach the pedals . . . as long as I didn't tell my mother. I always did eventually. He knew I would, but not before we had the fun of having a secret.

To get on the swinging bridge we had to climb up boards

nailed on the tree like an entrance to a treehouse. The first time, I was so scared my skin felt too tight, but I would rather have fallen in than tell my father.

Oh, sure, climbing to the top of the Statue of Liberty, the Eiffel Tower, was exciting, but if you want a real thrill, I know where there is a swinging bridge. I only take certain people and it's a test.

Think about a new way to look at the familiar. Change the reader's perspective as Carl Sandburg did when he saw Chicago as "city of the big shoulders." Quaint seacoast villages with weathered shingle houses proliferate in Maine settings. That's why we still read nineteenth-century writer Sarah Orne Jewett. Notice how she gave us another outlook in *The Country of the Pointed Firs* with one word—*apprehensively:*

"On the lonely coast of Maine stood a small gray house facing the morning light. All the weather-beaten houses of that region face the sea apprehensively, like the women who live in them."

Train your eye to focus on details missed by others writing about the same scene. Norman Maclean knew Montana as Jewett knew Maine:

The canyon above the old Clearwater bridge is where the Blackfoot roars loudest. The backbone of a mountain would not break, so the mountain compresses the already powerful river into sound and spray before letting it pass. Here, of course, the road leaves the river; there was no place in the canyon for an Indian trail; even in 1806 when Lewis left Clark to come up the Blackfoot, he skirted the canyon by a safe margin. It is no place for small fish or small fishermen. Even the roar adds power to the fish or at least intimidates the fisherman.

Maclean wrote in a sound track.

All of the places you include in your memoirs will not be picturesque or good places to fish, however. Some will be "hellholes," "arm pits," "wastelands," but since others have rendered these pejorative descriptions trite and tedious, you will have to find a new way to express your disdain. Joan Didion states her attitude toward Las Vegas in the title *Marrying Absurd:*

> What people who get married in Las Vegas actually do ex-
> pect—what, in the largest sense, their "expectations" are—
> strikes one as a curious and self-contradictory business.
> Las Vegas is the most extreme and allegorical of American
> settlements, bizarre and beautiful in its venality and in its
> devotion to immediate gratification, a place the tone of
> which is set by mobsters and call girls and ladies' room
> attendants with amyl nitrite peppers in their uniform
> pockets.

I especially like the phrase "bizarre and beautiful in its
venality," not only for its alliteration, but for the paradox
of beautiful venality, which should seem absurd or self-
contradictory, but turns out to have a tenable and coherent
meaning. Later you will have the opportunity to practice
creating your own oxymorons.

Setting is more than the locale and period in which the
action takes place, however. Look at the space around you.
What would you need to describe to give a clear picture of
your surroundings and circumstance? Are you lying on a
bed covered with silk sheets, sitting in front of a fan in your
undershirt, staring at a blank page or computer screen at
dawn with your lover sleeping nearby on crumpled Snoopy
sheets? Five empty whiskey bottles under the bed is a story
in itself.

If you are one of those customers antiques dealers dread,
the kind who can't look at the Windsor chair and pine table
they have for sale until you describe in precise detail the
ones your grandmother used to have until Grandpa made
a little money and replaced the old things with a chrome
kitchen set ordered from Sears and Roebuck, maybe you'll
feel better if you re-create that room in your memoir. There
is probably a universal—or at least an American—theme
buried in your story about the furniture. I think it is called
the crack in the American Dream.

My father used to work at a huge rolltop desk with a
dozen cubbyholes, a drawer that locked with a tiny brass
key, and a secret compartment only he knew how to open.
One day he chopped the top off with an ax. He couldn't
spread out his papers, he said.

When we see a play or movie, the director uses props
like my father's desk, costumes, and scenery. So do writ-

ers, but they have to build the decor out of words carefully selected. Readers feel misled if you point to a red night-gown, a rickety rocker, a broken window, but they have nothing to do with the story or don't reveal something about the characters. If the ebony box inlaid with mother-of-pearl lying on your dresser has nothing to do with the incident you're recalling, leave it out, but if it should be a gift from the man you loved before you married Harry, and the nick in the side came from Harry's throwing it against the wall, use it. It is easier to describe the new master bedroom and bath with the Jacuzzi, wall-to-wall sea green shag carpet, and blue floral bedspread than to show jealousy, but probably not as important for your story. Forget the decorator's tour. Show Harry winding up for the pitch. A wise set-designer friend says he doesn't want an audience to leave a play he has done humming the set.

The main difference between memoir and fiction writers is, you're supposed to be telling the truth. East Texas for Mary Karr *(Liar's Club)* and Alabama for Truman Capote are as important as Wessex for Hardy. In regional stories, local color—landscape, dialect, and customs—is exploited particularly for its inherent interest and oddity. If you grew up in Texas, mind-movies from your past must feature horses and rodeos and men in high-heeled boots. In the Midwest where I spent my childhood, the weather and bugs determined our livelihood. We tried to protect our crops from hail and cutworms the way city people attempted to lock out robbers.

If your story happened in a Cincinnati suburb, but because the action never moved out of your head, it could have been Chicago or Cedar Rapids, don't waste time describing how much crabgrass grew in the yard.

Food can be a shortcut to setting. Say "lobster" and try not to think of Maine, "gumbo" without seeing New Orleans, "sourdough" with no Golden Gate Bridge in the background. Indigenous food or drink usually comes with built-in images. You can skip many of the details.

Don't forget the weather if rain, a full moon, humidity, played a role in your experience. "It was a dark and stormy night" has become a cliché because it created just the right mood for murder and mayhem.

Poet Pablo Neruda claims his country had an art for raining:

> Sometimes it rained for a whole month, for a whole year. Threads of rain fell, like the long needles of glass snapping off on the roofs or coming up against the windows in transparent waves and each house was a ship struggling to make port in the ocean of winter. This cold rain from the south of the Americas is not the sudden squall of hot rain that comes down like a whip and goes on leaving a blue sky in its wake. The southern rain is patient and keeps falling endlessly from the gray sky.

Some settings have such a powerful ambience, they create their own weather. The Pentagon, a hospital, a battlefield, a jail cell, city hall, a church, can dictate style, character, diction, and destiny. Try to recall how the environment of your story might have affected your mental, moral, social, and emotional response.

## SETTING

☞ It was the weather's fault.

☞ The tackiness was what you liked about the place.

☞ The room you shared with a sibling felt tight.

☞ It was off-limits when you were young.

☞ The smell was what you remember about the funeral home.

☞ The hospital bed had been designed for someone much larger.

☞ The prices on the menu took away your appetite.

☞ No one told you it was black tie.

☞ The last bus pulled away, leaving you in the baking sun, with blowing dust, barking dogs, and no one who spoke English.

☞ You thought it was the most wonderful city in the world. That was before you had seen Barcelona.

☞ When you returned twenty years later, the place hadn't changed, but you had.

☞ To others it was a refrigerator box. To you it was a hideout.

☞ When you entered the place, you could feel a physical as well as an emotional change.

☞ At night, when the lights were out, everything looked different.

☞ The air crackled with tension.

☞ If someone gave you a push, you could swing way out to the middle of the river.

☞ You looked at the public ancient ruins, but saw private rubble.

☞ Even the surgical instruments were dirty.

☞ You weren't expecting company.

☞ The first time you saw the ocean.

☞ Your first flight.

☞ Your first office.

☞ Your father built a tree house.

☞ Think of something that hasn't already been said about:

| India | Paris | New York |
|---|---|---|
| Peoria | the opera | Hollywood |
| Super Bowl Sunday | a safari | the Lincoln Memorial |

# Chapter 22
# Portraying, Describing, and Developing
## The Major Players

*No less a presence . . . was my
classmate in English 5, the future
writer G.W.S Trow; he was just plain
George then, but he was sharp as
a ferret—I feared his bite.*

—*"Slipped Away," John Irving*

This is the fun part. Now that you have decided whom to
include in your memoir, your mission is to make them
real—people who get head colds, lose their temper, love
raisin pie. Include the horns and the halos. We read about
other people's lives—their family, friends, and foes—hoping
to find they, too, have their ups and downs: compelling
fears, humiliations, regrets, layered in between the happy
days. Look to novelists for techniques in presenting people,
just as you did when you were developing a setting.

Of course, you may be thinking, But fiction writers create
their characters. I'm going to write about Charlie. He has

shared the same lumpy mattress with me every night for twenty-two years. I didn't make him up.

Don't be so sure. Has anyone ever seen your kids as adorable as you do?

At different times, Mother, my sister, and Ann—my friend since college—have expressed the same concern about meeting people I know. They all have said, in some way or another, that they never would be able to live up to the picture I had painted of them. We call it point of view.

I smiled the first time I realized neither my father, my former husband, Dannon, nor any of the significant men in my life had ever found my tendency to embellish them the least bit of a problem. We call that point of view, also.

Think about the people you know and understand best. How did you learn to recognize those you could depend on, come to see through their charm, gain respect for their common sense? We flaunt our autobiographies, sometimes unaware, by the choices we make in food, friends, lovers, homes, careers, the polling both, music, spending habits, the way we use our leisure time, even the clothes we wear.

My cousin Steve, a West Pointer, is a three-star general in the army and the son Mother always wanted. When he came to spend the weekend with her after serving in Desert Storm, she wanted him to wear his dress uniform with a chest full of medals when she took him to lunch where her friends would be. He wore civvies.

Steve won the stars by jumping out of airplanes with the Rangers, leading men in battle in Vietnam, being shot out of a helicopter twice, training the first women candidates at The Point, planning ground maneuvers in Desert Storm, keeping the peace in Somalia, and supervising the cleanup operation of Hurricane Andrew. We all brag about him outrageously, but he doesn't talk about his career very much. He reminds me of a scene in *Death of a Salesman* when Willy says Bernard didn't even say he was going to Washington to do business with a man who had his own tennis court. Charley said he didn't have to. He was going to do it.

When you begin to focus just on the choices of someone important in your life, you will realize you understand more about her than you had imagined. To show the reader what you know, be alert to how master storytellers and memoir writers you admire have done it.

The following is John Irving's description of his Exeter wrestling coach:

"On his rump, he could scuttle like a crab—his feet tripping you, his legs scissoring you, his hands tying up your hands or snapping your head down . . . [but] he was always gentle with you."

Fiction writers don't have dibs on the following techniques used to reveal character. They are the same methods you will want to employ to present the major players in your memories:

- ☞ what he says
- ☞ what she does
- ☞ what he thinks
- ☞ what others say about her
- ☞ what others think about him

You're probably smacking your head, saying, Why didn't I start keeping this darn notebook earlier? Not to worry. The really important things people have said are probably engraved somewhere in your memory. Perhaps the following will give you a trigger to open the box. Think about the person who said:

- ☞ I do.
- ☞ You're hired.
- ☞ You're fired.
- ☞ I don't have much to offer you now, but if you'll marry me . . .
- ☞ It's a boy.
- ☞ I never did really love you.
- ☞ I'm sorry, but I've met someone else.
- ☞ I'm sorry, but you tested positive.
- ☞ I'm sorry, but it's malignant.
- ☞ I'm sorry, but she didn't survive the surgery.
- ☞ I'm sorry, but we don't accept Jews/African-Americans/women/people over forty . . .
- ☞ I'm sorry, but we won't be able to get to your job for some time.
- ☞ I'm sorry, but the flight has been canceled.
- ☞ . . . has been elected president of the United States.

☞   The jury's verdict is . . .
☞   Would you like to be my best friend?
☞   Would you like to go steady?
☞   We would like to invite you to join . . .
☞   We have decided to accept your offer.
☞   Your . . . has been accepted.
☞   Your . . . has been rejected.

You have so many memories. I suggest you choose the one driven by the intensity for your feelings about the topic. Recalling significant things people have said years ago still makes my blood flow faster: When the committee for my orals had asked the final question, my adviser hugged me, in spite of my having perspired through my best suit, and said, "Congratulations, Dr. Stanek. What could ever scare you again?" They tell me my father smiled at Mother and said, "Isn't that the damnedest thing," and then he died. I'd give the advance for this book to know what he meant. I knew what he meant when my then husband said, "You will never forgive me, will you?"

Picture the scene when someone said something that changed your life. Describe not only what she said, but the expression on her face or her stance. Show the effect of her words on both of you. If her words are powerful, you won't have to say how she said it. " 'I'm going to kill you,' she said angrily" is redundant.

If you are writing a childhood memory about the day your best friend moved away, the day you thought your life was over, but she only seemed to be excited about stopping at the Grand Canyon as the family drove west, you might not remember her exact words. It is probably better if you only recall the gist of it anyway. Writers have to be selective. Most of us talk too much and say too little. Just put words in her mouth that will convey how she hurt your feelings.

Maybe your friend hugged you, but it didn't last more than a second. Actions can expose people as readily as dialogue, but it doesn't have to be dramatic action like pulling a child from the path of a speeding train. A wink can change destiny. Simple gestures like cracking one's knuckles or looking at the ceiling reveal attitude.

Thomas Hardy wrote a poem about the first time he kissed the woman who was to become his wife. She sighed. They did not live happily ever after. When Caroline Kennedy hadn't yet outgrown her tomboy stage, she met her elegant mother at a benefit. A reporter noticed Jackie fussing with her daughter's hair as she greeted her. Caroline jerked her head back. Enough said?

Picture the person you are portraying when you've been riding with him in a car. Does he drive with both hands clutching the steering wheel, with the fingertips of one hand, with his right hand on your thigh?

Manners tell. If someone blows his nose on his hostess's white linen tablecloth, his action will speak louder than any judgment you could pass on him. When a dinner guest asks me why I keep paper clips in my medicine chest, I don't want to let her out of my sight the rest of the evening.

What others say or think about the individual can help you to make your point. For example, if you recognized something in this person everyone else missed, or the talent or personality trait didn't surface until later, including their erroneous appraisal could be amusing or ironical. If you were dazzled by someone everyone tried to warn you against, their opinions could add poignancy to the situation.

At my unrelenting insistence, my father once hired a boy I was mad about to work in our greasy machine shop. The boy wore gloves. My father said the boy would never have a dime. From what I hear, he never has, but he had eyes the color of robin's eggs and he drove a hot rod with dual cams.

Their physical appearance or their clothes need not be important in portraying your people. But if I were writing about the boy who didn't want to get his hands dirty, his looks and his clothes would be essential to the story because, as a teenager, that is what attracted me to him. He was from California, and when the guys in southern Illinois were wearing overall pants, he was wearing the first pair of Levi's I ever saw—the kind that rode low on his hips and hugged his tight tush.

Don't bother telling physical details, especially the color of eyes or hair, unless it is relevant to the story. The questions about clothes and looks are: "Is there a need to know, and what do I gain by including the information?" If that man in the three-piece tailored suit you are married to was wearing high-water pants and white socks when you met him, you probably won't be able to resist including it. If you fell in love with him but worried about having children with noses as big as his, include the nose.

What you will try to do in your story is to make your water wet and your people breathe. Their attitude is as important as their words, deeds, and appearance. I have never met Anna Quindlen's father, but when she said he had raised her to talk back and to keep up, I knew him. Anna and I were both firstborn children. I bet she would nod if I were to tell her my uncle once said, "Your father says he doesn't want a boy because he hasn't realized you aren't one."

If you are a firstborn son and your father named you Joyce, you have another knot to untie.

The following suggestions might open a secret compartment in your memories that could help you to introduce us to the people who have played a major role in your particular life experience.


## REVEALING WORDS:

- ☞ When I played back to him what I had heard him saying, he said I had distorted his intentions.

- ☞ The drill sergeant said if all soldiers were like me, we wouldn't have a chance of winning the war.

- ☞ She said I wasn't a good lover.

- ☞ He said he was a leg man himself.

- ☞ She said she would rather walk home than ride with me.

- ☞ He said it made me look cheap.

- ☞ She said I had no sense of adventure.

- ☞ He told me I was his favorite.

- ☞ She said I was too young.

- ☞ He called me a sissy and a crybaby.

- ☞ She said let's stay home and play Pick-up Stix.

- ☞ He said we can't invite them. It would be bad for business.

☞ She asked me why I didn't try to do something about my clothes.

☞ His bragging, even about me, embarrassed me.

☞ According to her, nothing was ever her fault.

☞ He said he would help me.

☞ She said I could do anything.

☞ He was the only elected official to whom I was tempted to write a masher note.

☞ She said I got what I deserved.

☞ He said . . . made him do it.

☞ She said I passed my affection around like a football.

## REVEALING ACTIONS:

☞ His generosity exceeded his means and my comfort level.

☞ She dotted her *i*'s with happy faces and used hearts for *o*'s.

☞ He never paid a bill on time.

☞ She always wore black, even in the summer.

☞ After she took him away from his first wife, she always seemed anxious.

☞ The presence of children made him uncomfortable.

☞ She always took the largest piece.

☞ He seldom returned phone calls.

☞ She never wrote a thank-you note for the gift.

☞ His driver's license was revoked.

☞ She never paid her share.

☞ His secretary chose the gifts he sent.

☞ She sighed and shook her head. A slap would have hurt less.

☞ He didn't believe in allowances. He preferred begging.

☞ She squeezed my hand to give me courage.

☞ He played footsie with me under the table.

☞ She winked at me.

☞ He held my hand, but he wasn't my date.

☞ She wanted to close the drapes so others couldn't see in. I wanted to open them so I could see out.

☞ He sent me postcards from places he knew I would sell my soul to see.

# Chapter 23
# Show, Don't Tell

*My mother never forgave my father*
*for killing himself, especially at*
*such an awkward time*
*and in a public park,*
*that spring*
*when I was waiting to be born.*

—*"The Portrait,"* Stanley Kunitz

Would you rather go on a safari where you hear the lions roar and feel the ground shake under a herd of elephants' feet, or have someone tell you how exciting a safari is? If you had a choice, would you prefer to feel the president's firm handshake or have someone who did tell you it was thrilling? Which would you enjoy more—tasting the hunks of dark chocolate and pieces of candied cherries in a pint of Ben & Jerry's Cherry Garcia ice cream, or reading the ingredients on the container? You can take your reader with you on that safari, let her feel the president's presence and his clammy palm, sample the surprises in the ice cream, if you show her what you saw, felt, and tasted.

Granted you'll find it easier to say you worked for the most egocentric, eccentric nincompoop in the State Department than show what an egotistical, erratic dolt he could be, but your reader will be more apt to agree with you if you let her decide for herself. Telling is like bossing someone around. Showing compliments the person you're trying to persuade.

To show your boss's self-centeredness, re-create a situation wherein his actions displayed his stinginess, such as when he took credit for work you sweated over for three months. To reveal how all his brain cells weren't on go, repeat something bizarre he said, like. "I have evidence Chelsea's cat wears a wire."

If he had a creepy tic or habit like twisting his hair or scratching his crotch, use it. Think about his tastes. A fetish for lime Jell-O with little marshmallows could have implications. At fifty-five years old, still living with his quite healthy mother raises questions about arrested development.

Readers prefer to make their own judgments. If you tell them your brother was a good sport, the response is "Prove it." Catch him in the act. Saying you married the most handsome man in the world won't do. Show them his thick hair the color of maple syrup, his infectious grin that crinkles his tanned skin. Let them decide.

You can tell me your uncle is the funniest man alive, and I might nod absently, but if you want me to slap my leg and chortle, have him perform. Let me hear him telling a story and see his droll demeanor.

When playing opposite Hugh Grant, British actress Emma Thompson, who found him "repellently gorgeous," wrote in her diary: "Why did we cast him? He's much prettier than I am." In our pasts we all have had our self-images squashed in comparison to someone else's beauty. Mine was my high school friend Carole. If you say your cousin Irene was so gorgeous she made you feel like a frump, I recognize the feeling, but don't see her attractiveness. I'll probably picture her tall with proud posture, hair dark as the queen of the night, periwinkle eyes, and a small nose that had never been broken, not even once. That's what Carole looked like. If your cousin had buckeye brown eyes and hair the color of old bricks, you will have to show me her picture for me to admire her too.

If you go back home, and want your readers to see the quaintness of the town, show us the barber pole, the brick streets, the benches in front of the bank where people loaf. Introduce them to the cobbler who wears a leather apron and repairs saddles as well as your Mary Janes. Order a green river or an egg cream for them at the drugstore.

When I was a child, Andy sold hamburgers for a nickel in a little hole in the wall where my father didn't seem to notice only men sat on eight backless barstools. He took me with him. The burgers were about as big around as the bottom of a Coke bottle, and Andy squashed them flat over a pile of onions sizzling in hot grease. I always ordered five. My father called me Wimpy. I was chubby. So was Andy. He wore a long white apron wound round and round.

When you stop the action of your story to tell the reader what furniture occupies a room, how to feel about the person, it's as if a playwright jumped on the stage in the middle of a performance to explain his set and characters. Those interruptions usually start like: "There was a . . ." "She had . . ." Let's assume the furniture is an important part of your memory. You, the narrator, can show the scene without stopping the flow. Let the reader experience the situation with you: "I was appalled by the clutter, as I maneuvered between a chair spitting its stuffing, a couch stacked with outdated newspapers, and Chinese take-out cartons caked with dried soy sauce. Five cats slept on the mattress on the floor. I held my nose, which objected to a litter box that surely hadn't been cleaned in this millennium. Sadie herself could have used a good soak in the tub."

How would you show the following situations?:

## SHOW, DON'T TELL:

☞  Dad was angry.

☞  Mom was sad.

☞  Sissy was mean.

☞  Nicholas was slow in school.

☞  He was sullen.

☞  She was grouchy.

☞ He was a flirt.

☞ She had thick lips.

☞ He had a bad complexion.

☞ She was a show-off.

☞ He was persuasive.

☞ She was a spendthrift.

☞ He was a worrywart.

☞ She was out of control.

☞ He was known for his bragging.

☞ She had interesting bones and weird eyes.

☞ He had an ungainly body structure.

☞ She had a bad attitude.

☞ The dog was a mixture of breeds.

☞ There was a desk, a chair, and a broken window.

☞ The closet was a mess.

☞ The food was unappetizing.

☞ The sex was boring.

☞ At night we played games.

☞ Ours was not a happy family.

☞ The road was slick.

☞ The caviar tasted funny.

☞ It was a good hamburger.

# Chapter 24
# Adding Details

*There were rows and rows of hams and sausages of all shapes and colors—white, yellow, red and black; fat and lean and round and long—rows of canned preserves, cocoa and tea, bright translucent glass bottles of honey, marmalade and jam. . . .*

—Confessions of Felix Krull:
  Confidence Man, *Thomas Mann*

Lance Morrow wrote his memoir, *Heart*, after he had had two heart attacks and two bypass operations. When I saw the review, I thought, Who wants to read about sickness? I don't want to read about that. But then I saw his phrase "my jalopy of a heart." He hooked me.

No one knows for sure how many books have been written about Abraham Lincoln, but one estimate says at least seven thousand. As a child growing up in the town boasting of the state house where, while serving in the senate, he is alleged to have jumped out the window rather than cast the deciding vote to move the state capital to Springfield, I thought I had heard every anecdote. But in his biography David Herbert Donald concentrated on Lincoln

**142**

before he became a saint. One of Donald's details I especially remember: Lincoln first declared his candidacy for the Illinois senate before he owned a suit.

Selecting vivid, colorful, revealing details will be one of the most important elements in making your memoir uncommon. Pay unwavering attention to the particulars of everyday life, such as morning noises: coffee perking to the rhythm of a TV correspondent's recounting the number of dead in a terrorist attack, the dog barking to go out, the paper landing with a thud on the porch.

If it's the forties, one of the paper's headlines could have been describing the hardships of Joseph Brodsky's childhood, but note how he uses details about tinned meat to tell his understated version in his short memoir, *Spoils of War:*

> In the beginning, there was canned corned beef. More accurately, in the beginning, there was a war, World War II; the siege of my hometown, Leningrad; the Great Hunger which claimed more lives than all the bombs, shells, and bullets together. And toward the end of the siege, there was canned corned beef from America. Swift, I think, was the brand name, although I may be wrong; I was only four when I tasted it for the first time.
>
> It was perhaps the first meat we had had in a while. Still, its flavor was less memorable than the cans themselves. Tall, square-shaped, with an opening key attached to the side, they heralded different mechanical principles, a different sensibility altogether. That key, skeining a tiny strip of metal to get the can open, was a revelation to a Russian child: we knew only knives. The country was still nails, hammers, nuts, and bolts: that's what held it together, and it was to stay that way for most of our lives.

All writing books will tell you to use concrete details and images, as Brodsky does, but the denotation of *concrete* rings so hard and sharp, it seems to rule out "an apricot chiffon negligee." Think: real, tangible, material, solid. Rather than saying your first boyfriend was homely, show us his skinny neck with an Adam's apple the size of a Macintosh. If you go out for dinner, tell us if you had ham hock and beans or oysters on the half shell. Don't simply read a book, read *Tropic of Cancer*, *The Iliad*, *Franco: A Biography*.

Let the reader gorge on nuggets of shared memory, whether it be cars with rumble seats, silk stockings held up with garter belts, your mother's crockery, the mayor's reputation, the number one song on the Hit Parade, the best of the Beatles, or the Glenn Miller song you always danced to.

A reader's reaction to a flower garden can be "ho hum," but the one where your grandmother would only allow plants promising to produce pink blossoms—or your mother-in-law's, with flowers as formal as soldiers on a reviewing field—shows character.

You know your iguana, pig, monkey, or kissing fish has a personality as distinct as your kids', but you'll have to give particulars if the rest of us are to understand.

Horses are my animal of choice, and since stabling one on my New York terrace seems not to be a nifty choice, I haven't had a pet for years. Then I met Elise, who lives with my friend Mira in Maine. I feel perfectly silly about the mushy feelings I have for that big bear of a dog. She's a classy Bouvier des Flandres, the breed that look as if they're wearing a Persian lamb coat. Elise has terribly proper manners, except when a seagull swoops anywhere near the deck, and she goes ballistic until her foe is out of range. No one knows the origin of her mania against the birds, but after an outburst she always looks troubled as if she would like to talk to a dog shrink. Oh, I know she can't talk . . . sort of . . . but when I ask her if she wants to go with me for a walk or in the car, I swear I hear her say, "Wait until I ask Mira." Then she trots off, stands patiently at her mistress's feet until permission is granted. Thanks is said with a rub of her curly head on Mira's knees before this genteel lady scampers toward the door like a frisky puppy. Sometimes I swear she says, "Okay, we're out of here."

Some clothes have made a lasting impression. Did your first suit come with two pair of pants, both of which scratched, or did your mom insist, because you were growing so fast, you take the one with the jacket sleeves so embarrassingly long, you appeared to have no hands?

Anyone who thinks writing about haircuts would be trivial hasn't had to live with a hideous one. Hair is a literary symbol of strength. Why else would you have pitched such a fit the first time you were taken to the barber or beauty shop? That flashback should not be in black and white. How did the clippers feel on your neck? How did the hair tonic smell? What kind of chair did you sit in? Who took you, Mom or Dad? Were they proud or embarrassed by your behavior, the result?

Remember the dime store you haunted when you were nine? Frederick Busch says, "The kid [Busch] . . . will make that journey past the Woolworth's that sells lead soldiers and smells of heavy cloth sold from rolls and from the polish applied to its wooden floors."

When you were married, did he wrap five carats of marquise diamonds all around your finger, or do you wear a plain gold band with a tender message engraved inside? Did you marry a woman who was apt to have someone come to the house to wax her legs, or one who waxed her own floors with a thick yellow goo demanding a lot of polishing?

Write with your nose, your ears, your eyes: the sound of glass breaking in the night, perfume smelling as if something has died on her neck, a car with baby bootees hanging from the rearview mirror.

Maybe a place—like the bridge for Maya Angelou or the death camps for Wiesel—has played such a significant role in the part of your life you have chosen to write, it will be your focus and a structuring device. The details you choose to show such a pivotal place will be especially critical.

In a memory about the death of her father, see how Kitty Flury uses a house for her focus in "Ticky-tacky" for the "Thoughts of Home" column in *House Beautiful*. Notice the explicit details she brings to show you the house:

> I remember everything about that house. We bought it for $5,500, and the monthly payments were $66. Our phone number was 5851. There were thirteen steps up to the attic. A spirea bush grew at the southeast corner. The dog next door was named Skippy. I kept my colored drawing pencils in a little blue box my mother gave me that still held the scent of Bluegrass soap. The neighbors were the Fizmaurices, the Macks, the Vincelettes (they were from France),

the Perciantes (they were from Canada), the Worshels, the Sawyers. Wild strawberries grew in the vast woods out back. My father paid me a penny for every gypsy moth caterpillar I picked off the willow tree we planted. . . . Buying the house was the central event of my childhood. It was an expression of faith. My father was ill—he had a damaged heart, the legacy of rheumatic fever when he was a child—and the house meant that we believed he would get better.

Describing places, where mountains, an ocean, cornfields, or thirteen steps to the attic can set them apart, is easier than describing people. Everybody has a couple of ears, and unless nature has played a dirty trick, mouths and noses sit in about the same place on all of us. I often make subway riders uncomfortable, staring at them, trying to determine what details I could use to show how their faces are so alike, but so different. Mouths make a difference: Little tight ones with narrow lips you wouldn't want to kiss seem to be opened by a spring.

Hemingway didn't have a reputation for giving credit to people who helped him, like Maxwell Anderson and Gertrude Stein or competitors like Fitzgerald. The exception was Sylvia Beach, who ran a bookstore and rental library in Paris called Shakespeare and Company. For the terse writer who did not trust adjectives, Hemingway's description of Beach in *A Moveable Feast* could be called extravagant:

> Sylvia had a lively, sharply sculptured face, brown eyes that were as alive as a small animal's and as gay as a young girl's, and wavy brown hair that was brushed back from her fine forehead and cut thick below her ears and at the line of the collar of the brown velvet jacket she wore. She had pretty legs and she was kind, cheerful and interested, and loved to make jokes and gossip.

I have trouble visualizing the haircut, but the "pretty legs" gives the description a Hemingway brand.

Retrievals of a lost time are achieved by the evocative detail. Everyone's mother had a kitchen, but you probably didn't always get a whiff of nutmeg in theirs. And who besides your mom alphabetized her spices, for pity's sake?

In my family I have cousins galore with enough eccentricities and endearments to fill volumes. This manuscript had already gone through copy editing when Stu was killed in a car accident. Stu was the youngest, the handsomest— the cousin who made me laugh. He won four major letters his freshman year in college, batted 510 one season, and sang the lead in *The Music Man.* After he and his college sweetheart married and had three sons, they still looked at each other as if they had a secret, but whoa . . . even if I felt in our family the best had been saved for last, no one was going to believe this portrait. He seemed too good to be true. Stu had an ironic sense of humor. I could especially see the mischievous grin on his face.

I had to add details to make Stu seem real . . . his hair . . . of course. His outrageous hair wasn't perfect. He had a mop of it that grew straight up as if all the energy in his athletic body had activated his head. Then he insisted upon that silly, 1890's middle part which didn't do a bit of good. Maybe after I've achieved a little distance, I'll find something else, but I doubt it.

Search the repository of your memory for the particulars of the following that would make your experience and the people you know different from any other's.

## ADDING DETAILS

- ☞ A parade
- ☞ Your mother's sewing box
- ☞ The most contrary car you ever owned
- ☞ Something had died in the attic
- ☞ The prettiest dress you ever had
- ☞ The river at sunrise
- ☞ The best garden you ever planted
- ☞ The ugliest person you've ever known
- ☞ It was the custom in their country
- ☞ A golf partner from hell
- ☞ Your child's favorite toy

☞   The boss's desk

☞   A bathrobe you can't give up

☞   The dress you wore to your junior prom

☞   Your high school band uniform

☞   It was a flop

☞   A strong-willed child

☞   A scary ride

☞   An objectionable drunk

☞   A misunderstanding with a person you loved

☞   White-water rafting

☞   A broken leg

☞   A houseguest who stayed too long

☞   Your squash partner's style

☞   A piece of jewelry you longed to own

☞   The room where you spent the first night of your honeymoon

☞   A love child

☞   His teeth

☞   Her knees

# Chapter 25
# Language

*Nor use too swelling, or ill sounding words.*

—Ben Jonson

Language, obviously, is the basis for everything we have already discussed: keeping a notebook, creating a setting, describing someone, adding details. However, especially if this is the first time you have attempted to put those remnants of your past on paper, the urgency and the earnestness of your task has probably caused you to include a few clunkers, say more than you needed, be too formal or serious, or try too hard to be funny. By focusing on language, you will have two purposes: to clean it up and to be more creative, goals that are not contradictory. It is time to take off the headphones to hear what you have said, and to hone it with a sharper pencil and a good eraser, but it is also time to play with the words.

If *playing* sounds too frivolous for what you have in mind, think about T.S. Eliot—bank clerk in his wire-rim eyeglasses—the soberest of men. His Prufrock measured out his life in coffee spoons and worried about the Eternal Footman holding his coat and snickering. *Snickering* is such a delicious word, so much more delectable than giggling, tittering, snorting, or laughing.

Don't always settle for the first word to pop into your mind. Look for shades of meaning. Let's assume you start to write "John smiled at me." Picture the scene. Did he smile or was it a grin, a smirk, a sneer, a leer? Did he beam or simper?

Picture the difference if that beast of a boss scowled, frowned, glared, glowered, grimaced, or pouted. Did he have a tendency to cavil, carp, or quibble?

When your seventeen-year-old son felt good about himself, did he swagger, strut, sashay, or stride around the house? When the boy sunk ten points in the tight fourth quarter, did his father bluster, boast, or brag?

Remember the kid who always told the teacher? Did the little sneak squeal, tattle, or blab? If he grew up and was hired in your office, does he still inform, disclose, reveal, or gossip?

I like the shenanigans *wiggle, wobble, wangle,* can perform. Their sound is impish. They could worm their way into some tomfoolery. In your notebook I hope you have been collecting tangy, tasty words and phrases, and you have been listening for those with zest, zip, and heft, especially action verbs.

Cooks and writers have a lot in common. They have discerning knowledge of ingredients—some magic ones—like what to add to a pie crust to make it flaky. A good chef knows when to sprinkle a little salt (but not too much), when to garnish, and when to let his creation speak for itself. A touch of nutmeg, cinnamon, oregano, or basil can spice up a bland concoction, but a heavy hand with the red pepper or garlic can drive diners from the table.

Making it clear comes first, but also touching the heart and/or the mind makes the difference between a flaky or a soggy story.

A couch is just a place to sit until a writer tells you some lasting aroma of the buried life still clings to the tumbled cushions.

The chairman of a large corporation under attack showed he had wit as well as troubles when he told a reporter, "Getting information out of me is like trying to frisk a seal."

After a midterm election, a reporter provided a fresh way to look at what happened when he said, "The results of the election shattered the wall of invincibility around the Republicans."

When I was having Chapter Eleven dreams after buying the house in Maine, a friend sent the Oscar Wilde line: "Moderation is a fatal thing. Nothing succeeds like excess." However, even a rascal like Wilde would not have said excessive language succeeds. He makes his point with a statement as lean as a long-distance runner.

We will begin with the eraser. If you do not agree writer's bloat has reached epidemic proportions, you have not been reading letters from the IRS, your lawyer, or your child's school.

## WEASEL WORDS

I borrowed "weasel words" from Ken Macrorie (whose book *Writing to Be Read* has been a staple in my library since the sixties) because it is such a perfect metaphor, I could not think of anything more appropriate. A weasel is an animal whose earthly purpose no one has been able to determine, and the verb weasel means to be evasive or deliberately misleading like the mumbo jumbo my mother used to receive from Medicare.

Our speech is crawling with weasel words heard so frequently, "by the way," recognizing them can be "sort of" a problem, but if we don't, it can "kind of" cause us trouble with an editor, although it is "probably" a "relatively" minor part of the editing process unless weasel words are a "particularly" good example of what he most abhors.

Useless words in trite expressions have become locked together in our speech and writing. Word wasters tend to say "in many instances" when "often" will do, or "in the capacity of" and "in respect to" rather than "as." Pry apart the following and any others you can spot:

☞ absolutely complete
☞ final conclusions

- ☞   limited amount of space
- ☞   repeat again
- ☞   owing to the fact that
- ☞   same identical
- ☞   personal friend

We also have a tendency to attach unnecessary prepositions to verbs:

- ☞   clean out the closet
- ☞   pour in the gin
- ☞   sweep up the kitchen
- ☞   find out the answer
- ☞   use up the rest of the soap
- ☞   dry out the towel
- ☞   come across a word
- ☞   play around with the computer
- ☞   wash down the walls
- ☞   tie up the horse
- ☞   dress up the doll

That useless word *that*, creeping into places where it isn't needed, annoys me the most. (My students say I have a fetish.) Notice how it defuses the impact of the following:

- ☞   I told her that I wished she would die.
- ☞   He gave the impression that he was lying.
- ☞   I thought that I could do it without her help.
- ☞   Joe wrote that he was deserting the army.
- ☞   The doctor assured me that I would live.
- ☞   That boy is heading for trouble if he doesn't stop that.

*Which* is another word a writer should have to have a prescription to use. *Which* works well for a pedantic text striving for a precise definition like: "A symbol is anything which signifies something else; in that sense, all words are symbols." But in your memoir, "The house in which I live is in shambles" is cumbersome. "My house is in shambles" works better.

## ACTIVE AND PASSIVE VERBS

Writers with a good ear for language and a sense of humor tend not to be so hard on politicians' gutless talk. Picture "The orders came from above." I will forever see little Ollie North, in a marine colonel's uniform too big for him, reaching up to the sky and waiting for orders to take over the country to come floating down to him. "The letter was dictated" also tickles my ribs. With no one around performing the act, I try to imagine the shorthand scribbles appearing magically by an invisible hand, or an eerie voice coming from no speaker finding its way on a tape.

"For the good of all Americans, it has been decided . . ." taxes will be raised, some public servant's salary will be raised, a social program will be whacked. We know we have been hit in the stomach, but have no idea whom to punch in return.

In the memoir, there is nowhere to hide. You are the actor. Whether you feel you escaped or deserted your family, you did it. The reader will be more apt to empathize if you say so rather than concocting a cop-out like "The decision was made to leave."

The passive voice—sort of—legitimately allows one to express ideas without attributing them to a specific personal source. Government agencies, bureaus, departments in corporations—places where opinions and policies supposedly come from consensus—claim the passive "A decision was reached" to be appropriate. However, the grammatical camouflage usually represents moral weakness. Someone does not want to accept the responsibility for his act, deed, or words. "It was rumored that Henry was dipping into the till" is the coward's way. The person you trust says: "I have been told Henry was dipping into the till." Think of the times you've heard, "It is the opinion of the firm" rather than "I think." Who is the firm, for Pete's sake?

Strong active verbs give your work oomph. Assume you witnessed a crime. You say, "He slashed her throat." The reader sees the act and winces. "Her throat was slit" slows the pace, weakens the effect.

Action verbs not only vitalize an image, but can provide sound effects. Assume you're writing an anecdote about having to give someone a shot. Your verb choice will modify the picture and set the tone: She screamed, howled, wailed, shrieked, screeched, or squawked. Notice how the sounds of the words resemble the sounds they describe. Just the clatter the verb *squawked* makes diminishes the gravity of the situation. (See "Onomatopoeia" in the following chapter.)

## DANGLING MODIFIERS

Passive verbs can cause other problems. Dangling modifiers appear to modify the wrong words or they have nothing to modify, as with the use of the passive verb in the first example:

☞ To lose weight, whipped cream should be avoided. (To lose weight, John should avoid whipped cream.)

☞ Moving to Alaska, his asthma got worse. (After moving to Alaska, he realized his asthma got worse.)

## MISPLACED MODIFIERS

Even an elegant detail placed where it seems to modify the wrong word can spoil the effect, creating confusion or even humor. Adjectives usually precede the words they clarify. Adverbs are more flexible in their placement but should be as close as possible to the words they modify.

☞ She says she means to leave the country in the first paragraph. (She says in the first paragraph she means to leave the country.)

☞ He played a great part in the war with Japan as a statesman. (As a statesman, he played a great part in the war with Japan.)

## ADJECTIVE OOZE

If two similar adjectives are used, either one will probably produce a stronger effect than two together: "her dark, black hair." Cluttering the image with adjectives defuses and confuses: "her smooth, dark, black, straight hair cut short in a slick Juliet cap with stubby bangs."

If two phrases say the same thing in different ways, the effect will be strengthened by choosing the better of the two and dropping the other: "For Beryl, going to college was like being born again, getting a second chance."

## CIRCUMLOCUTION AND EUPHEMISM

The bureaucrats in Dickens's satirical Circumlocution Office were masters at using the passive voice. Specializing in obscuring the truth, they drove the characters in *Little Dorrit* to distraction, but the practice didn't end with the Victorian Age. Look at those in our society who find circumlocution a pleasant detour around a disagreeable idea. As we go to press, "downsizing" takes the blue ribbon for dodging. Note the roundabout way to say someone is lying:

"She shows difficulty in distinguishing between imaginary and factual material."

But the best of the worst is:

"Now for a brief message from our sponsor." The plug following the fib is neither brief nor a message, but a pitch.

If your memoir includes an episode about having to terminate the employment of someone, just fire him. If he swept the floors and emptied the trash, call him a janitor, not some kind of fake engineer.

The psychological principle that an unattractive or frightening idea can be made pleasant by calling it something else doesn't work. I don't cotton to going to my final rest, passing on, meeting my Maker, kicking the bucket, and especially not receiving my just rewards, any more than I do dying. Euphemisms can be effective if you are presenting a person who uses them in a character-revealing way. You will never have to say your cousin Millie is prissy if she calls manure "plant food," and says she has to go do-do when she is going to the toilet.

Whitewashing works better on fences.

## HONESTY

Years ago, from a source I can no longer locate, I read a short memoir by Elizabeth Hardwick written after she and Robert Lowell were divorced. A friend asked her if she were lonely. "Not always," she replied. I have never met Elizabeth Hardwick, but I would trust her.

Frank Kermode resigned as editor of *Encounter* magazine when he discovered the money for the magazine came from the Central Intelligence Agency. In his memoir, *Not Entitled*, he said about his involvement:

"The worst of it was that while I did not know that I was invited to play the part largely because I was thought to be safely inadequate to it, I could wake in the night and suspect that it was so."

In a more playful tone, Robert Lipsyte remembers the way a boy actually felt about having to face a bully. "I hated getting beaten up. I hated having friends feel sorry for me, hated feeling my scabs harden."

The phoniness shows when a writer is faking emotions she doesn't feel to impress, please, or cover up. The bogus sentiment reads as sentimentality or frigidity.

Being candid about the facts as well as the feelings is also the easiest way to do it. Liars have to have such good memories.

## POMPOSITY

I once had a colleague, desperate for tenure, who must have spent the night before faculty meetings searching the dictionary for grand words to impress the chairman. Lincoln was better at it. "Pejorative" was one I remember because my associate used it often and not always appropriately. Once after he said he had a strongly pejorative response to changing the time for our next meeting, the droll chairman said, "Paul, does that mean you're agin it?"

Memoirs work best when they are clear and honest. If you reach for highfalutin language hoping to make people think you are intelligent, it can backfire. Readers could think you're being pompous or hiding something.

I don't remember where I read about the difficulty the Federal Bureau of Standards had communicating with a foreign-born plumber who was using hydrochloric acid to clean clogged drains. They sent several memos like: "The efficacy of hydrochloric acid is indisputable, but the corrosive residue is incompatible with metallic permanence." The plumber kept pouring the hydrochloric acid. Finally someone wrote: "Don't use hydrochloric acid. It eats the hell out of the pipes." I would read his memoirs.

*Ersatz*, one of my favorite words, can lose its firepower if used too often. I reserve it for something really fake like the ersatz elegance a decorator imposed on the lobby of our apartment building, which now reminds me of a Queens funeral home.

I like the sound of *superfluous*, but it is one of those words that calls attention to itself, like a bright scarf on a black dress. Displayed too frequently, it lives up to its meaning. *Needless, useless, excessive*, blend better.

## REDUNDANCY

I recently had lunch with a young woman who told me, "My boots are from Paris. They're French."

In an attempt to make themselves perfectly clear, even presidents have been known to say absolutely ridiculous things. Watch out for adverbs. They can call attention to your lack of confidence about what you are saying. The *perfectly* and *absolutely* in the preceding sentence diminish rather than emphasize the impact.

I'm glad I saved *superfluous*. Here is a good place to use it:

| | |
|---|---|
| rich billionaire | cruel killer |
| wet rain | marathon race |
| baby doe | |

The ear can hear what the eye cannot see. I have no idea why, but it is true. Test it. Read your memoir aloud and you will find repetitions, redundancy, dissonance, you have missed. If you find a sentence that makes you stumble, run out of breath, or mispronounce a word, rework it. Your reader will trip on it too.

The opportunity to read aloud to others makes the strongest case for joining a writers' workshop or group. In my classes someone constantly slaps her head and says, "I can't believe I said that! I read this over three times before I came."

Develop a safecracker's ear for the useless, the burdensome, and the boring language that clutters your work. Follow George Orwell's advice: When you can cut a word, cut it. Actually, he said "cut out," but since he didn't need the preposition, I cut it.

People see the words with their eyes, but they hear the sound and rhythm. When you read your work aloud check the following:

☞ Listen for the boring pattern of too many sentences following the same structure, and try to rearrange the order. However, take care not to shift the focus or relinquish logic for variety. For example, "Wringing the chicken's neck and putting him in the frying pan, Mary sat down to read her Bible" sounds as if Mary did all acts simultaneously.

☞ If you were trying for a soft sound, but the words clamor and yell, check the thesaurus. Pay special attention to verbs. They do the hard labor.

☞ Editors screech if you split infinitives such as: I want to quickly pay this bill. (I want to pay this bill quickly.)

☞ Unless you're using them to show character, mimic, or create comic effect, don't forget the passive-voice verbs go with the rest of the deadwood. You might as well clean them out now. Eventually an alert editor will shoot them back to you.

# Chapter 26
# Figurative Language

*The only credential the city [New York] asked was the boldness to dream. For those who did, it unlocked its gates and its treasures, not caring who they were or where they came from.*

—Act One, *Moss Hart*

Figurative language intentionally departs from the normal order, construction, or meaning of words in order to gain strength and freshness of expression. Figures of speech have the ability to create a pictorial effect, describe by analogy, or discover and illustrate similarities in otherwise dissimilar things.

## METAPHOR AND SIMILE

In a short story showing how a young boy looked at a girl, Ring Lardner said:

"He gave her a look you could have poured on a waffle."

Figurative language does not belong to fiction writers alone, however. In a commencement speech at Howard University, General Colin Powell said:

**159**

"African-Americans have come too far and we have too far yet to go to take a detour into the swamp of hatred."

In his memoir, *Speak Memory*, Vladimir Nabokov wrote: "The cradle rocks above an abyss, and common sense tells us that our existence is but a brief crack of light between two eternities of darkness."

All three men made their points imaginatively by creating a metaphor, an implied comparison. The formal literary definition for the metaphor is: A word that in ordinary usage signifies one kind of thing, quality, or action is applied to another, without the express indication of a relation between them.

Even Aristotle praised the metaphor as "the greatest thing by far" for the poet because it permitted him to find the similarities in seemingly dissimilar things. But I was surprised when I began to notice metaphors in the usually stuffy financial reports coming across my desk: "While economic tailwinds have blown somewhat harder in recent months, they are hardly gusting."

When Israeli Prime Minister Rabin was assassinated, soldiers and politicians called him tough and brave. His young granddaughter spoke of his ability to love and comfort. The fitting metaphor for those born in Israel, like Rabin, is Sabra, a fruit with a prickly outside and a sweet interior.

Russell Baker's proclivity for using animal metaphors to describe politicians has been making readers smile over their morning coffee for years. I remember a column called "Snouts in the Slop." He often uses variations of hogs at the trough and rats leaving a sinking ship.

Kitty Flury said, "My parents waited ten years for me: That's the way they always put it, as if I were a train to a place they desperately wanted to go."

Everybody in our building looked the other way as long as the Bird Lady kept her winged friends confined in her apartment, but then she began to feed the pigeons on her windowsills, and they used ours as a pissoir. "Pigeons are rats with wings" became my favorite metaphor.

When you are trying to describe a situation, place, or person essential to your story, think comparison—something enough like it to be credible, but different enough to be intriguing. Anna Quindlen said she received the most mail ever after she wrote a column about waking up to find her sturdy three-year-old in red pajamas standing by her bed. She compared him to a fireplug.

If Quindlen had said her son looked "like" a fireplug, she would have created a simile. Metaphor implies the comparison. A simile uses *like* or *as*. Shakespeare said Macbeth's "title hangs loose about him, like a giant's robe/Upon a dwarfish thief." But it is more important to be able to originate metaphors and similes than to know their definitions.

However, mixing metaphors creates confusion and often amusement, rather than clarification. The following appeared in an article in the *Los Angeles Times* about the constitutionality of a proposition:

"The court doesn't need to look at any particular sections, because they fall like dominoes rather than each being a duck having to be hit with a round of buckshot."

One of my students put his friend Henry in a tricky situation when he said, "Henry shot from the hip and didn't pull any punches."

Just the phrase *dead metaphors* sounds so gross, no wonder mixing them as the writers above did "cooks their goose." Dead metaphors and similes are those clichéd comparisons so common, we use them without being aware they are figures of speech: "frog in my throat," "big as a barn," "handwriting on the wall."

Recognize the dead ones, and don't try to revive them. Wallace Stevens said, "Life is the elimination of what is dead."

## PUNS

In three previous books, I have taken a prim position on puns. This time I've decided to tell the truth. Some puns are irresistible. *First Knight,* the movie about Lancelot's carryings-on with Guinevere in Camelot, touched my funny bone. I read an article in the business section of the paper simply because of the headline, WHO HAS BEEN EATING YOUR NEST EGG? Then there was the Italian immigrant who, having not yet mastered English, marked a videotape: "Rally at Crazy Mention." His supervisor finally translated. It was a "Rally at Gracie Mansion." The same wordsmith twister recorded an oxymoron as a "nazi moron."

Writers often use puns in book titles, like Twain's *A Tramp Abroad,* and *ME ME ME ME Not a Novel,* by M.E. Kerr. I especially appreciated the irony in former Russian ambassador Anatoly Dobrynin's, *In Confidence,* a revealing account of the Cold War and his involvement.

Shakespeare was such an incessant punster, scholars are still quibbling over the origin of some, such as when Hamlet is asked where Polonius's body is. He replies:

"A certain convocation of politic worms are e'en at him. Your worm is your only emperor for diet: we fat all creatures else to fat us, and we fat ourselves for maggots."

Elizabethan critics argue the "worms" refers to the Council, or Diet, of the City of Worms that pronounced Martin Luther an outlaw. Professors win or lose tenure and prestige over such arguments, but Samuel Johnson said punning was Shakespeare's "fatal Cleopatra for which he lost the world, and was content to lose it."

The play on words in a pun, based on the similarity of sound between two words with different meanings like wait/weight, wrap/rap, son/sun, can be amusing, but as with any figure of speech, too many can spoil the effect, and some are just too silly, like "the lesser of two weevils."

Never trust "no pun intended."

## SYMBOL

We find symbols in every sphere of intellectual activity from the simple to the most complex. On the most elementary level, a symbol is a concrete object to which some abstract and usually emotive significance is attached. Think of the furor when a national flag or a cross in a church is desecrated. Words are symbols that refer to material things, but their reference is to something abstract: meaning. Paradoxically, symbols both embody and conceal meaning. For example, a crown is the symbol of a king's authority, but nothing about it relates to its meaning. Therefore, the relationship between the symbolic object and its significance is arbitrary and dependent upon something other than the qualities of the symbolizing object. Think about the bridge between the white and the black communities in Maya Angelou's hometown. The bridge itself was simply a means of getting across some water.

A symbol that taxes the imagination takes time and space to develop. I suggest you avoid the obvious—the rose as a symbol of beauty, dark clouds as a symbol of trouble. Effective symbols weave their way into a story, sometimes without the writer even being aware she has created them. Faulkner died swearing his bear was just a bear. Everyone believed him as much as they would have Twain's telling them the Mississippi was just a river. But if something continues to appear in your memories—a piece of jewelry, a statue, a blanket, a rock, the Joker—it might have significance beyond what is apparent. When a symbol appears naturally, it enhances, but when you try to slap one on for effect, usually it doesn't become a beauty mark.

## OXYMORON

When hardly anyone without a degree in English knew how to spell or pronounce oxymoron, it was my favorite member of the poetic language family. Recognizing one was like knowing a secret code. Then Madison Avenue discovered it and spoiled the word's uniqueness by overexposure in a wretched ad. The figure of speech that means bringing together two contradictory terms, like "repellently gorgeous," "refashioned reality," "absolutely normal chaos," "killing for peace," still creates a sharp emphasis, but the word itself has had the life punched out of it. One could say oxymoron now has a "dim sparkle."

## ONOMATOPOEIA

Try to say "hiss" without hissing. There you have it. Onomatopoeia is the literary term for the use of words that imitate the sounds they make, like *buzz, rustle, swish.* Tennyson often exploited the device in his poetry (sometimes too much): "The moan of doves . . . and murmur of innumerable bees."

## ALLITERATION

For those of us who would rather play with words than shoot at things on Nintendo, alliteration—the repetition of sounds in successive or closely associated words or syllables—is the dangerous figure of speech. Resisting them is as difficult as passing up popcorn at the movies. My notebook abounds with combinations like: "fettuccine and fusilli," "kamikaze kissing," "master manipulator," "prickly pear," Painter Bacon's "gilded gutter life." I included a reviewer's remark when she said *Loose Lips* would be a good title for a memoir she felt had been written for revenge. Alliteration enhances as long as you don't overload or sacrifice sense for sound.

One of the most effective is from the credo of Adolph Ochs, who purchased the *New York Times* ninety-nine years ago: "To give the news impartially, without fear or favor, regardless of any party, sect or interest involved."

## ALLUSION

Faye Dunaway titled her memoir *Looking for Gatsby*. Robert Lipsyte said Willie, the bully in his junior high, "was Grendel." Allusion is a figure of speech that makes a casual reference to a famous historical or literary figure or event. Shakespeare said, "I know not where is that Promethean heat/ That can thy light relume."

I especially like one that comes from an alleged story about a prisoner of war whose mail was censored. He is alleged to have written to his wife he felt the same warm affection for his captors as the people in Atlanta felt for General Sherman. The censors let the remark go through.

## PERSONIFICATION

The old song "The Little White Cloud that Cried" gave human characteristics to a cloud, personifying an inanimate object. Personification is a figure of speech used not only by poets like Keats who endowed a Grecian urn with mortal form, but frequently in television ads, such as allowing finicky cats to talk. I especially like Stanislaw Jerzy Lee's "No snowflake in an avalanche ever feels responsible."

Common sense advised.

## MALAPROPISM

Every writer deserves to have one family member descended from Mrs. Malaprop. In Sheridan's play *The Rivals,* Mrs. Malaprop was constantly giving vent to such expressions as "illiterate him, I say, quite from your memory," or "as headstrong as an allegory on the banks of the Nile." In her honor, we have the figure of speech *malaprop*—an inappropriateness resulting from the use of one word for another that has some similarity to it. My friend Judy's boss provides her with gems like: "We must put our heads to the grindstone." If you are fortunate enough to know an heir of Mrs. Malaprop's, carry your notebook and be sure to include her in your memoir.

While you are doing something else, you might do the following exercises for the left hand:

## FIGURATIVE LANGUAGE

☞ With the aid of a simile (like or as), make a comparison:

> your goldfish
> your junk drawer
> your family reunion
> your first pony ride
> the first snow
> heavy makeup
> Cousin Charlie

☞ Use a metaphor to imply a comparison with:

> your gerbil
> your relationship with your father-in-law

your first cup of coffee in the morning
quitting smoking
exercising
writing a memoir
firing an employee

☞ Create an oxymoron to express your conflicting feelings about:

duct tape
fax machines
lawyers
romance novels
peanut butter
Aunt Clara
the Boston shuttle

☞ Make a pun out of:

a ruler
a bun
a fan
a bat
jerk
boil
stamp
kite
chief
yolk

☞ Turn the following into pleasant and sensible alliteration:

baseball game
brickbat
chimes
Bible school
daughters
your dog
polo ponies
Internal Revenue Service

Use just a pinch.

# CHOOSING A TITLE

Titles sell.

As hard as you have worked, don't quit with the winner's circle in sight. Find a title you will be proud of, one that is perfect for what you have to say. Wall Street would call the title a "leading indicator" of your memoir's worth. Whether your purpose is to market it to a publishing house, a magazine, a quarterly, or your family, if the title is awkward, confusing, cute, silly, or difficult to pronounce, it will work against you.

After creating memorable titles like *A Streetcar Named Desire, Cat on a Hot Tin Roof, The Glass Menagerie,* Tennessee Williams's calling his memoir *Memoirs* still amazes me. It's like naming your son Boy or calling your dog Dog.

If the Rolling Stones had called themselves the Rolling Pebbles and Madonna's name were Mary Jane, I wonder if fame would not have alluded them.

Some titles themselves tweak one's interest by suggesting a story:

Soon after Dylan Thomas had killed himself with drink at The White Horse Tavern in Manhattan and had been buried back home, his widow, Caitlin, left Laugharne, the Welsh village by the sea. She tried to commit suicide in London by leaping from a third-floor window. The next few months she spent detained in a mental home in Surrey. After her release, she went, with ironic intent, to the island of Elba where she furiously wrote an emotional response to Dylan's death. Her notes became *Leftover Life to Kill.*

Ilene Beckerman's life wasn't always as smooth as whipped cream either, but as her title, *Love, Loss, and What I Wore*, implies, she tells it in a lighter tone. Her style is more understated than the clothes she remembers wearing the day she decided to leave her second husband or the two blue dresses her father bought for her after her mother died—a few days before he disappeared and she never saw him again.

James Baldwin's title *The Fire Next Time* got everyone's attention.

Although *Not Entitled* does reflect British critic and teacher Frank Kermode's style of self-abasement, the text suggests several interpretations. Literally, the title was taken from a naval phrase stamped on a sailor's envelope when what he had been docked during a pay period exceeded the amount he was owed.

Ben Bradlee's title, *A Good Life*, also reflects the voice of his memoir, which a reviewer called feisty, cocky, and proud of his life, with *good* meaning both enjoyable and having made a contribution.

*Palimpsest*, Gore Vidal's title, sent me to the dictionary. I was convinced he had coined the word or was showing off by dipping into a foreign language none of us would recognize. But there it was, even in the old paperback Webster's I've used so long, it's now in two pieces. The definition corroborated Vidal's explanation of his erasing some but not all of the original while writing something new over the first layer. It's an honest, if obscure, title alerting us to how time affects and changes memory.

One couldn't get the joke of Shana Alexander's title *Happy Days: My Mother, My Father, My Sister & Me*, until one had read the book, resonating with the awesome power of withheld love by a cold mother. Alexander's father, Milton Ager, a Tin Pan Alley songwriter, inspired the ironic title. His most famous songs were "Happy Days Are Here Again" and "Ain't She Sweet."

I like tell-all titles such as *Bare Knuckles and Back Rooms,* by Ed Rollins, a former political adviser who had been brawling in back rooms for thirty years. Like many political memoirs, Rollins's story could also fit into the revenge category. He doesn't just pass out bouquets to the Republicans and brickbats to the Democrats, but pays back presidential candidate Ross Perot and New Jersey governor Christine Todd Whitman, whose campaigns he had left under unpleasant circumstances.

Titles revealing in advance what the plot entails are like being able to see previews for movies before paying your eight fifty.

Joyce Johnson, who was involved with Kerouac in the fifties, wrote a memoir about the women in the Beat Generation. She called it *Minor Characters.* Her clever title almost made me forgive her for snitching. She told us Kerouac, famed author of *On the Road,* did not know how to drive.

Psychiatry professor Kay Redfield Jamison's *An Unquiet MIND,* an account of her struggle with manic depression, which William Safire called the most emotionally moving book he had ever read about emotions, leaves no doubt what the reader is to expect. Nor does *Winter Light: Reflections of a Yankee Queer,* by John Preston, the memoir of a gay man who found a home—and himself—in Maine, but died of AIDS before his book was published.

*Jack and Rochelle* offers no preview. There are many holocaust memoirs, but, as a reviewer stated, few with the unflinching reportage of Jack and Rochelle Sutin, who wrote an accurate account of their lives that included intimate details like the way people who were crowded together in a hole in the earth managed to make love. The nebulous title, however, does not give a clue about demonic episodes such as when Rochelle, with others, beat five German prisoners to mush.

Michael Ryan's *Secret Life* should have a warning subtitle like: *The Confession of a Young Degenerate.* This mem-

oir is an arresting, but disturbing, portrait of his depravity
that begins with being molested as a child and continues
to chronicle his sexual experiences with the family pet, a
male teacher, female students, and an assortment of other
men and women who capture his attention.

There is pathos in Alfred Kazin's title, *Writing Was Everything.* The past tense says it all for a distinguished writer
who came of age in the 1930s.

*Our* is the operative word in *Having Our Say,* by Sarah
L. and Elizabeth Delaney, with Amy Hill. I don't usually
take seriously memoirs written "with" someone, but the
Delaney sisters were both over one hundred years old when
Ms. Hill helped them put together their remembrances,
which were so lively, their story became the basis for a
Broadway play.

I suppose after serving as press secretary to Presidents
Kennedy and Johnson, senator from California, and television news correspondent here and abroad, what came next
would be a postscript. Pierre Salinger called his memoir
*P.S.*

A straightforward title does not mean you have to settle
for something bland, boring, unbecoming. Truman Capote's *A Christmas Memory* tells you what to expect. I guess
it would have been presumptuous to have called it an *Un-
forgettable Christmas Memory,* but that is what it was for
me.

Biographers often effectively use subtitles to strengthen
their main titles, such as: *American Caesar: Douglas Mac-
Arthur, 1880–1964, The Dark Side of Genius: The Life of
Alfred Hitchcock.* Allusions to heroic figures and genius—
even the dark side—would appear arrogant in an autobiography or memoir; however, if your name is as familiar to
the reading public as Coca-Cola, you will not have to
bother about a title. Colin Powell's *My American Journey*
appears in type half the size of his name. David Brinkley's
name comes first, with *A Memoir* following in small letters.
If I had been Beverly Cleary's publisher, I would have put
the well-known children's book author's name in huge letters, hoping it would overpower *My Own Two Feet,* the title
of her remembrances, which I found flat-footed.

Although William Maxwell's *All the Days and Nights* is
billed as fiction, it reads more like a memoir about his

Illinois family who lived just a few miles up Route 51 from
mine. The title would have been ideal for memories, but
Maxwell has always blurred the lines between fiction and
memory, such as his mother's ill-fated brother and his gen-
tly self-deluding wife becoming not so fictional characters.
Many of his stories and nonfiction pieces are about the
same thing: the death, when he was ten, of his adored and
adoring mother in the influenza epidemic of 1918.

Maxwell is certainly not the only writer who turns memories into fiction. The idea to write this book surfaced in
Washington, D.C., where everyone has, or thinks he's had,
an interesting life, but especially in the nation's capital,
disguise prevails. Look at the number of novels featuring
a president with shifty, darting eyes, who sweats a lot
through a five-o'clock shadow trailing into a neck that dis-
appears like a turtle's. Philip Roth's *Our Gang*, published
in 1971 just before the Watergate break-ins, is still the
most scathing of the anti-Nixon spoofs. His loathsome protagonist's name is Trick E. Dixon. But even some of Nixon's
White House gang, who wrote a number of self-serving and
vendible memoirs after the president's resignation, also
wrote novels about the president, such as Spiro Agnew's
*The Canfield Decision* and John Ehrlichman's *The China
Card*. Their memoir titles, such as *The Haldeman Diaries:
Inside the Nixon White House*, were not remarkable, but at
least let people know what they were peddling.

Then there is *Maverick: A Life in Politics*, Lowell P. Weicker
Jr.'s memoir written with Barry Sussman. Since Weicker
did indeed wear nobody's brand, it's the perfect title, unfortunately perhaps the best thing about the book. Weicker
makes statements breaking with conventional wisdom that
deserve explanation, such as: "Gerald Ford ended up being
the best President in my adult lifetime." But Weicker did
not elaborate. Being a maverick works better in politics.
Readers do not like to be teased.

Keep in mind the purpose of a book title—to distinguish
and describe what you have written in an appealing and
attention-getting way. Originality and appropriateness are
the guidelines.

The following are favored references for writers in search
of a title.

## SOURCES FOR TITLES

☞ *Bartlett's Familiar Quotations*

☞ The Bible

☞ *The Oxford Dictionary of Quotations*

☞ *Home Book of Proverbs, Maxims and Familiar Phrases,* by Burton Stevenson

☞ Shakespeare

☞ Poetry

# BECOMING YOUR OWN EDITOR AND CRITIC

*Conception is much more fun than delivery.*

—*Georges Pompidou*

I think *boss* is a word and a concept devised by the devil. Listen to the hissing sound. Look at how short and cocky the word struts onto your page, as if it has a Little Caesar complex.

What I like best about being a writer is not having a boss, set hours, and a "reg" book. Who can be creative wearing shoes, panty hose, or a tie? When the ideas are flowing fast, an artist—painter, writer, musician—can catch them any way she is able, whenever she feels like it, and put them into whatever shape she comes up with at the time. Others call that a first draft. I call it freedom. But not even the birds can hang on to freedom. Stronger forces toss them around. They compete with peers as hungry as they are.

Even if no one more critical than your favorite grandchild or best friend will read your story, you will want to do revisions. Bring your work into the world with love, attention, thought, passion, and understanding.

Samuel Butler left good advice for a revision starting point:

> Think of and look at your work as though it were done by your enemy. If we look at it to see where it is wrong, we shall see this and make it righter. If we look at it to see where it is right, we shall see this and shall not make it righter. We cannot see it both wrong and right at the same time.

Common complaints about memoirs from critics are: dwelling too long on ghosts from the past, attributing unwarranted significance to casual occurrences, offering one epiphany too many.

Thinking like a writer has already sharpened your senses. I agree with the pundits who maintain writing cannot be taught, but I am certain craft can be learned and observation can be trained to be more precise, acute, and particular. I am also convinced you have learned to write by writing. It has been a process of consciousness raising, of becoming acutely aware of language, of an audience. The revision process won't be as painful as you might have imagined.

## FIRST READ-THROUGH

An editor's job is to assist the author in realizing the author's intentions. Since you are to play a dual role, you, the editor, will want to set guidelines such as the following for your, the author's, first reading:

- ☞ What did I want to say?
- ☞ Did I begin with the interesting part?
- ☞ Is everything related to my original intention?
- ☞ Are the people alive?
- ☞ Have I always shown time and place?
- ☞ Have I given explicit examples, added details to make the incident clear?
- ☞ Does it flow?
- ☞ Does it add up?

☞   Did I say it honestly?
☞   Did I get it said/do what I promised?

## SECOND READING

Close your study door or go to the park. People who talk to themselves can be considered dangerous, but reading your work aloud again is a necessary step. You will hear things you didn't see and hear things you missed previously. That's a promise. Now is the time for line editing, a word-by-word examination to see what is imprecise or irrelevant.

☞   Listen for boring repetitive sentence patterns.
☞   Check adverbs—the better you write, the fewer you'll need.
☞   Eliminate the second adjective when one will do.
☞   Be certain you have used powerful verbs. Rewrite to eliminate linking verbs—is, are, was, were—when a strong verb will create a more powerful image.

Removing the clutter will improve the pacing.

## GRAMMAR

Inspect your work for agreement of subjects and verbs, tense, and case. Remember prepositions take an object: "The news must remain between you and me" (not "you and I"—a frequent error).

Invest in a grammar handbook if you are not certain about punctuation, such as using an apostrophe with the possessive case: "John's coming at this time worries me."

## TONE AND VOICE

Consistency is the key. You don't want to sound like Nor-

man Vincent Peale on one page and a sob sister on the
next.


## AUDIENCE

Writing can, and should, have a cathartic effect for you,
but your intention should be to create something to *move*
readers, not to expose them to what you think will be good
for them. Remember Salinger's Quiz Kids in the Glass family stories, who imagined the Fat Lady? Visualize your audience. If they begin to cough and squirm, revise.

Writing is not thinking out loud—it's the result of silent
thought that will bring the reader to the same conclusions.


## REPETITION

Telling the reader what you have already told him is boring.
If you explain on page one your pony was a pinto you
named Spot, no need to remind her of his splotches on
page ten.

Do not use the same word more than once in a sentence,
and not in the same paragraph or page unless there is
absolutely no way out.


## CLICHÉS

"Sharp as a tack," "quick as a wink," "smooth as silk,"
"green as grass," "nipped in the bud," began their pervasive journey into the language as fresh images, so visual,
so economical, they became popular and overused until
they're now as wilted as last week's roses, but harder to
spot. Examine your work carefully. Find the clichés. Treat
them with the same loving tenderness you would
cutworms.

Poet Muldoon has great fun with clichés in *Symposium:*
"You can bring a horse to water, but you can't make it
hold its nose to the grindstone and hunt with the hounds."

## CLARITY

---

Whoever said, "If I had more time, I would write less" was a wise person. Too many details can create a muddle. Continuing on after you have reached your destination is a waste of time for you and the reader. Make it clear and concise, like "I have a dream."

I hope yours comes true.

# MEMOIRS AND SOURCES

## Memorable Memoirs

Michael J. Arlen, *Exiles*
Nicholson Baker, *U and I*
Russell Baker, *Growing Up*
Truman Capote, *A Christmas Memory*
Colette, *Sido*
Roald Dahl, *Boy*
Elizabeth Eisenhower, *Breaking Free*
Vivian Gornick, *Fierce Attachments*
Moss Hart, *Act One*
John Houseman, *Run-Through*
Mary Karr, *The Liar's Club*
Suzanna Kaysen, *Girl Interrupted*
Alfred Kazin, *A Walker in the City*

Frank Kermode, *Not Entitled*
Wayne Koestenbaum, *The Queen's Throat*
Stanislaw Lem, *Highcastle: A Remembrance*
Willy Morris, *My Dog Skip*
Vladimir Nabokov, *Speak Memory*
V.S. Pritchett, *A Cab at the Door*
Carolyn See, *Dreaming: Hard Luck and Good Times in America*
Wilfred Sheed, *In Love with Daylight—a Memoir of Recovery*
Kate Simon, *Bronx Primitive*
Art Spiegelman, *Maus*
Henry David Thoreau, *Walden*
John Updike, *Self-Consciousness*
Eudora Welty, *One Writer's Beginnings*

## Sources for Publishers and Agents

*Literary Market Place*
*Writer's Market*

LOU WILLETT STANEK, PH.D., has taught at the University of Chicago, Marymount Manhattan College, and the New School for Social Research. She is the author of *So You Want to Write a Novel, Whole Language,* and three novels for young adults, and has contributed to numerous magazines, journals, and newspapers. She is a member of PEN and lives in New York City and Bailey Island, Maine.